MAKING
HEIRLOOM
BOXES

MAKING
HEIRLOOM
BOXES

PETER LLOYD

THE GUILD OF MASTER CRAFTSMAN PUBLICATIONS

This book is dedicated to my wife Christine. With love.

Loads of thanks to: Andrew Crawford for his generous sharing of knowledge; Alastair in the camera shop for his help;
Val Corbett for her generosity with her fantastic tree pictures; my sons Mark and Thomas for their willingness to help me
move wood when they'd rather be doing something else; Stephanie where's-my-book Horner for her patience;
Paul Richardson for telling me I could do it; and Pam Grant for her encouragement and the very first article all those years ago.

First published in 2002 by
Guild of Master Craftsman Publications Ltd,
166 High Street, Lewes,
East Sussex, BN7 1XU

Reprinted 2003, 2006, 2010, 2014

ISBN: 978-1-86108-176-6
A catalogue record of this book is available from the British Library

All photographs by Peter Lloyd except:
James Arnold-Baker: Hilary Arnold-Baker's box on p 164
Anthony Bailey: pp 37, 38, 46, 54, 62, 74, 89, 90, 104, 119, 120, 134, 149, 150 and 156
Bob Barrett: Chris Cantwell's boxes on p 165
Blantern and Davis: Martin Lane's box on p 165
Val Corbett: Figs 0.1, 0.2, 0.3 and 0.4 on p 1, pp 36, 88,
Andrew Crawford: pp 166, 167
Terry Evans: p 166
Daniel Guilloux: Jean-Christophe Couradin's boxes on p 164
David Haas: Michael J. Brolly's box on p 166
Mike Hemsley FBIPP: Clare Vetterlein's box on p 164
Robert Ingham: p 166
Ross Kaires: p 164
Kim Kelzer: p 164
Paul Kodoma: Edward L. Love's box on p 165
William Lemke: Tom Rauschke and Kaaren Wiken's box on p 165
Po Shun Leong: p 166
Hap Sakwa: Charles B. Cobb's box on p 164
Chris Skarbon: pp 6 and 24
Sborisov/iStock/Thinkstock p 118
1stphotoiStock/Thinstock p 148

Publisher: Jonathan Bailey
Production Manager: Jim Bulley
Managing Editor: Gerrie Purcell

Colour illustrations by Simon Rodway
Black-and-white illustrations by John Yates

Designed by Mind's Eye Design, Lewes
Cover design by Graham Willmott, GMC Design Studio
Typefaces: Goudy and Avenir

Colour origination by Viscan Graphics (Singapore)
Printed and bound in China

CONTENTS

INTRODUCTION

Boxmaking began for me with a piece of wood. A fairly large bulk of wood in fact – about 10in wide, 12in thick and 4 or 5ft long (0.25 × 0.3 × 1.2–1.5m). It was burr oak and 'would I like it for school and how would I like it cut?'.

It happened at the sawmill, whose main business was making pit props for the mining industry. Its offcuts were sawn up for firewood and it was for firewood that I was there. But I couldn't just fill the trailer with firewood and leave. There was wood everywhere. A huge stack of tree trunks stood piled in a great pyramid and a hydraulic crane dumped them onto rollers where they were manhandled and levered into position and then fed into a giant band saw.

This was all new to me. I knew the theory of converting trees into wood but to see it in real life provoked a mixture of feelings. Those trees had stood proud and living in the countryside for hundreds of years and more. They'd been a home to thousands of animals and stood firm against countless gales and storms. Now they were dead, in a heap, awaiting their turn for the saw. I know it sounds sentimental, even slightly ridiculous, but that was the feeling the trees provoked. However, alongside the sadness there was an excitement. There was new life. As the trees were squared-off on that band saw, suddenly I stopped seeing dead tree and started seeing wood. Swirling figures and rich colors held me spellbound.

There are two points at which wood looks its best: when it is freshly cut and when it is finally finished. At all the stages in between it can look gray, dirty and boring. So, when I was offered a large bulk of burr oak, how could I refuse? 'Three-quarters of an inch', (19mm) I said in a snap decision. Suddenly I had the responsibility of owning eight boards of gorgeous burr oak. Too wet to do anything with of course, so I carefully stacked them and filed them away in the to-do-something-with-sometime section of my mind.

Time passed, I changed jobs, worked abroad for a couple of years, returned home and was determined to work for myself. But doing what? I unearthed that burr oak, 10 years on, and it was certainly dry, but the $\frac{3}{4}$in (19mm) was now $\frac{5}{8}$in (16mm) in places and the planks were as kinked and buckled as sheets of scrunched-up paper. There wasn't a lot I could do with it, but the thought of it wouldn't go away – it was just too good to ignore. Even with my tiny workshop – a shed in the garden – it was some time before the idea of boxes occurred to me. I'd made one before so why not use the burr oak? And why not use the waney edges as a feature on the lid? So my first box was born. A friend saw it and said she'd like to buy it. To buy it! To pay money for it! I was thrilled and my new career – Peter Lloyd, boxmaker – was underway.

Some of the projects in this book are boxes which I have made several times. They are almost stock items. In these cases the photos should more or less match the words. Other projects are very much one-offs in that I was commissioned to make a box which I photo-graphed and made notes on as I went along. For these, I made only one box so if I goofed and had to make another lid or a new set of hinges, the photos might look slightly out of kilter. And if I got to a point in the box and thought 'why didn't I do that earlier', the text will say do it but the photos won't show it done.

While we're on the subject of photos, things have changed during the writing of this book. I have to confess it has taken me a lot longer than it should have. I'm older now, maybe a little wiser, and I've certainly got several more machines. In fact, when I bought a table saw I had to completely reorganize the workshop. Some books give the impression of having been written over a weekend; this one certainly wasn't, so if you spot any anomalies in the photos, add time to the equation and they should make sense.

Fig 0.1 *Glencoyne, Ullswater, Cumbria, UK*

Fig 0.2 *Lone tree, Buttermere, Cumbria, UK*

Fig 0.3 *The raw material*

Fig 0.4 *Freshly cut wood*

Fig 0.5 *Hydraulic crane moves the trees from stock to saw bench*

Fig 0.6 *Handling the split log*

Fig 0.7 *Cutting for pit props*

Fig 0.8 *Sawyer guides the wood through the band saw*

Fig 0.1
Fig 0.2
Fig 0.3
Fig 0.4
Fig 0.5
Fig 0.6
Fig 0.7
Fig 0.8

SOURCING AND SEASONING WOOD

I'm often asked where I get my wood. The sawmill is one source, where I buy my wood green, otherwise I buy it from various wood dealers, in which case it is usually kiln-dried and ready to go. A lot of wood suppliers will do mail order, but would you buy a second-hand car that way? Actually, it's not that bad.

SOURCING

Finding wood suppliers isn't difficult. The listings at the back of woodworking magazines are a good start. Finding 'reputable' suppliers is more difficult. If you can, ask your friends, colleagues and other woodworkers for recommendations. Building a working relationship is a good idea but the wood supplier does *want* to sell wood.

Buying wood *is* a bit like buying a second-hand car. You don't know much about the inside workings of the thing, you kick the tires a bit and think it looks fine but do you really know that it hasn't been clocked, welded back together, and had its gearbox filled with sawdust? In the end you have to trust the seller a little, try to make an informed judgement and hope to goodness he's slightly less ignorant than you.

I still use my 'original' sawmill; it is trying hard now to diversify as the market for wood mining props is declining. The piles of ash, oak, beech and elm are still there and so is the excitement. I still love to see the freshly cut wood as it falls from the saw and to visualize turning it into boxes.

SEASONING

Wood needs to be seasoned before it is used so that its moisture content doesn't alter too much when the finished piece is placed in a different environment – someone else's house. If there was a significant change, the wood would move; it would cup or twist or both, causing the wood to split and joints to blow apart.

If wood is too wet when it is used, it will shrink as it dries out, which will probably cause splitting. Antique furniture tends to suffer from this if it suddenly finds itself in a dry, centrally heated environment.

Briefly, seasoning wood brings its moisture content into balance with that of its environment. As air circulates around the wood, moisture gradually passes from the wood into the air until the moisture level in each is about the same. In kiln-dried wood this process is speeded up through the addition of heat. If the wood happens to be *drier* than the air around it, moisture passes from the air into it until their levels are the same.

Green wood

If I am buying wood green – that is, freshly sawn – I first put it 'into stick' in the garden. I have the wood sawn into 1¼in (32mm) boards and stack these with ¾in (20mm) 'sticks', placed around 16in (40.5cm) apart, to separate each layer of wood from the one above. This allows the air to circulate around each board, and the drying to occur more uniformly. I stick with the custom of laying the boards following the order in which they were cut. I then cover the stack with pieces of old corrugated iron to keep the worst of the rain and sun off, and leave it for a minimum of one year. After this I bring the stacks in from the garden to the workshop and leave them, still in stick, for another year or so. During this time I monitor them, measuring their moisture content every three to four months with a moisture meter, and write the reading and the date onto the board.

Usually, what happens next is that I cart these boards off to a large joinery shop where I plane and thickness them to around 22mm (⁷⁄₈in). (I know I've suddenly switched from inches to millimeters; raw wood seems to suit inches while finished wood seems happier in millimeters – don't ask me why.) I then stack them, without sticks, in the work-shop where I keep a dehumidifier going most of the time; I also use a hygrometer to keep an eye on the relative humidity. Once again I write the moisture meter readings onto the board, checking every three to four months. After about six months, if the reading on the top board hasn't changed, I 'map out' the box, cut it roughly to size and put it to one side yet again for a further couple of months. By this stage the wood is about ready to be made into a box.

Kiln-dried wood

When I buy the wood kiln-dried, the process can be cut considerably. I still leave it for a while, cut up into box sizes, and keep an eye on it with the moisture meter: sometimes wood bought from a wood supplier is dried too much and needs to go the other way. My overriding principle is that the wood is stored in a place where the relative humidity is normal, that is, between 40% and 60%.

Fig 1.1 *Pyramid of hardwood logs waiting for their turn on the saw*

Fig 1.2 *Stocking wood 'in stick'*

Fig 1.3 *Wood stacked inside a kiln*

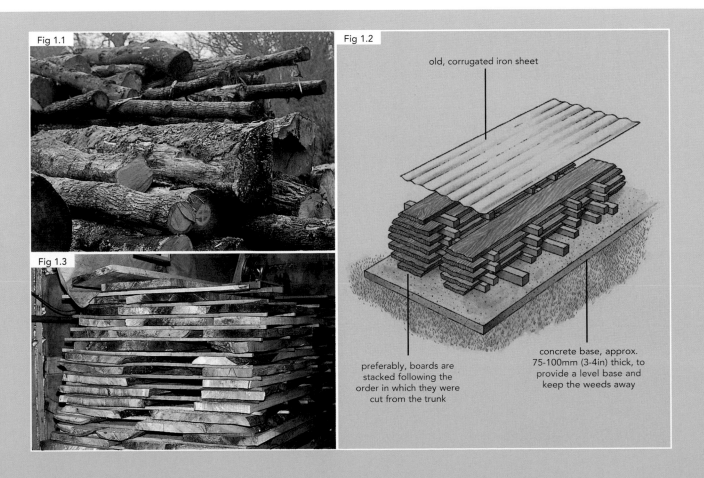

Fig 1.1

Fig 1.2

Fig 1.3

old, corrugated iron sheet

preferably, boards are stacked following the order in which they were cut from the trunk

concrete base, approx. 75-100mm (3-4in) thick, to provide a level base and keep the weeds away

TOOLS AND EQUIPMENT

The information in this section is not prescriptive. It is in no way meant to be a list of tools that you must own before you can make a box. In fact, my first box was made with a few hand tools, a bench with a vise, a router and an electric drill with a foam drum sander. Boxes can be made in the tiniest of workshops with the minimum of tools. Machines can wait.

HAND TOOLS

Sharpening

A sharp plane or chisel is a joy to use and the difference between singing off shavings with a sharp blade and forcing a blunt blade through a piece of wood is enormous. It's possible to write a whole book on sharpening. I shall simply describe here how I do it.

I sharpen all my blades on two oilstones. One is a man-made stone with two faces, coarse and medium, and the other is an old stone which I acquired second-hand a long time ago. It is very fine and looks a little like slate. With the blade clamped into a honing guide, I use the medium oilstone first and then the very fine. For an extra sharp edge I strop the blade on the leather wheel of a sharpening machine. With plane irons I maintain just one bevel and on chisels I have a 30° honing angle. For me, a blade that will cut when it is pushed against the edge of a piece of paper is sharp.

Chisels

A set of four good chisels would be $\frac{1}{8}$, $\frac{1}{4}$, $\frac{1}{2}$ and $\frac{3}{4}$in. My chisels are constantly in and out of their spring clips, which I keep on the wall near the vise. In addition to the more usual sizes, I've got a $\frac{1}{16}$in chisel, which is very useful for cleaning up tiny dovetails or squaring the ends of small routed grooves, a $\frac{1}{2}$in paring chisel, which can be handy for jobs where you need a long reach, and a 1in chisel which is good for cleaning up larger areas. It's definitely worth paying a little more for a quality set: good-quality steel will keep its edge much longer.

Planes

For a long time I had only one plane – an old Record 04$\frac{1}{2}$ – and I made this do for everything. I've since picked up a second-hand try plane which is very useful for planing the bottom of boxes as it can span the width of the box. In the same way it is also invaluable for planing the joint between the lid and box when the lid has been sawn off. I was also very happy to be given my father-in-law's Norris smoothing plane one Christmas. It can be a little short for planing a long length, but I seldom do. A block plane is occasionally useful, particularly for end grain, although I must confess that I tend to reach for the switch on the sanding disc – now that I have one – before picking up the block plane.

Surforms

Surforms come in all shapes and sizes. The one I find most useful, known as a surform standard plane, is two-handled and has a curved blade. Also available are surform block planes, round files, shaver tools, flat files and planer files. All have replaceable blades and, with a good, sharp blade, will remove wood quickly.

Fig 2.1 *My planes – the surform at the front followed by the seldom-used block plane, my smoothing plane behind that and my beautiful Norris on the left. And don't laugh at my old wooden jack plane. I still use it; it's very satisfying and very good at getting through wood pretty swiftly*

Fig 2.2 *My two oilstones, Eclipse honing guide and Tormek grinder*

Fig 2.3 *Sharpening a chisel*

Fig 2.4 *If you can push the blade through paper, it's sharp*

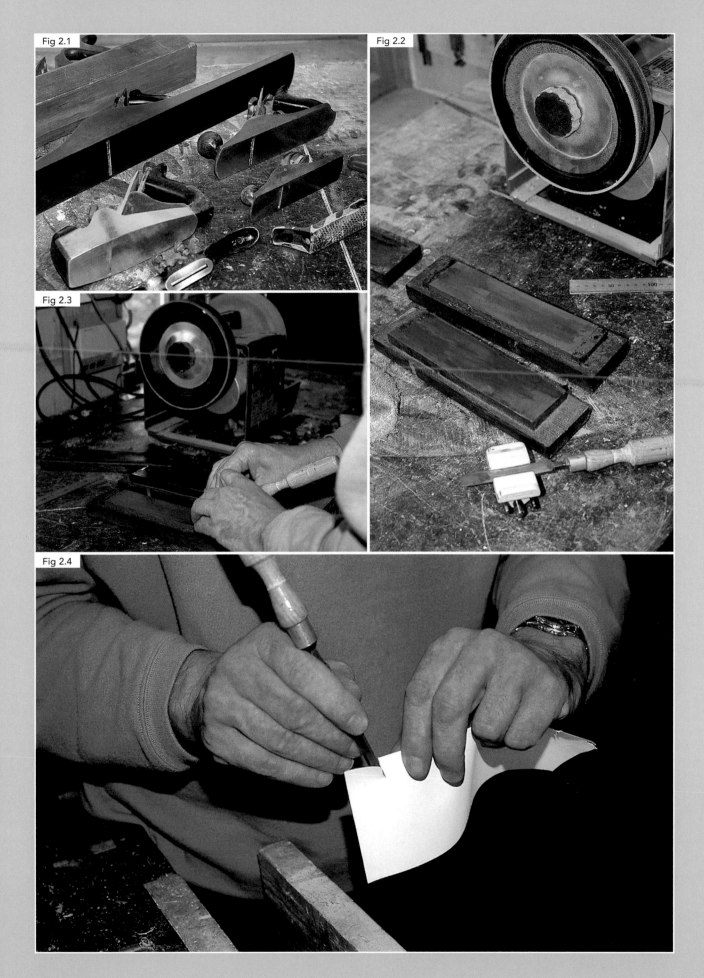

Fig 2.1

Fig 2.2

Fig 2.3

Fig 2.4

Files

A selection of small files is handy – a round, a triangular and a couple of flat – more for use on the metal in jigs than for boxes though.

Rules and squares

A zero-ended 300mm (12in) steel rule is a must. A 600mm (24in) version of the same thing is useful. A good 150mm (6in) try square is essential and again, a larger 300mm (12in) version is worth having.

On the subject of squares, a squaring rod is easy to make and repays the 10 minutes it takes many, many times over. Such a rod is simply a length of material – in my case 5 × 10mm ($\frac{1}{4}$ × $\frac{3}{8}$in) in section and about 600mm (24in) long – with a pointed step at one end.

Sliding bevels

A sliding bevel is handy if you are marking out and cutting dovetails. A purpose-made dovetail square is very useful.

Vernier calipers

My latest measuring stick is a pair of digital vernier calipers. It is 150mm ($6\frac{7}{8}$in) long, reads in millimeters or inches at the touch of a button, and is accurate to $\frac{1}{100}$ of a millimetre or $\frac{1}{1000}$in. It measures internally, externally, and into holes, and is hardly ever off my bench.

My delight in them has led to slightly obsessive behaviour; I spent some time recently trying to adjust a jig so that it was spot on – too much time. In the end I had to tell myself, rather sternly, that the amount I was trying to correct was about half the thickness of a human hair.

Knives

A knife is almost essential for accurate marking out; a shoulder line marked with a knife is so much easier to chisel to than a pencil line.

Humble pencils

I'm sure my workshop has a black hole into which pencils fall, never to be seen in this space/time continuum again. I tend to use soft pencils for rough marking out and propelling pencils with a 0.5mm lead when I want to mark something accurately.

Saws

A backsaw and a coping saw are the bare necessities; a fine dovetail saw is very useful. Ripping by hand is something which I have always tried to avoid but if it has to be done, a good, sharp ripsaw will do the job, and with that extra sense of satisfaction that a table or band saw just doesn't give.

Vises

A vise has got to fall under the heading 'essential'. A woodworking vise flush with the top and edge of the bench and with hardwood cheeks has got to be one of the very first tools into the workshop. The larger the better really. Mine is an old Record 53½ with 10in (254mm) jaws. It opens to 10in (254mm) which is quite adequate. Its quick-release mechanism is a boon, saving time and hassle. A tail vise complete with stops can come later. My own is home-made and very basic. I often wish that I had a proper one.

Sandpaper

There's a vast range of sandpaper available these days, little or none of which is made with sand. I use aluminium oxide paper for both machine- and hand-sanding. I sometimes start as coarse as 40 grit and work through 80, 120, 180, 240 and finally 400 grit.

Clamps

There's a very old adage – you can never have too many clamps. And you can't. However, you can get away with just a few. I built up my collection slowly.

Fig 2.5 *Squares, rules, squaring rod, bits of wood used for 'spacers' and vernier calipers – they're digital and they're brilliant*

Fig 2.6 *A fantastic amount of pressure can be exerted using sash clamps; my home-made ones are gradually being replaced by all steel*

Fig 2.7 *My selection of clamps*

Fig 2.5

Fig 2.7

Fig 2.6

HAND-HELD POWER TOOLS

Sanding tools

Foam drum sander

This was the first power sander I owned. It is a hard foam drum that attaches to a power drill. To sand a perfectly flat surface with a foam drum is virtually impossible, a fact which I'm sure had a considerable influence on the way my boxes have developed their soft, flowing lines. Using a range of grits (from 60 through to 400) and sanding with the grain, it's possible to achieve a very good finish. The major drawback with a foam drum is dust. Without a full-face air filter, the clouds of dust in a small workshop are very unpleasant.

Random orbital/rotary sander

This machine is a great stride forward from the drum sander, mostly because it extracts dust via holes in the abrasive disc. It can be connected to the workshop extraction system or to a small, portable vacuum unit; the dust is drawn through the body of the machine and into whichever system is used. The model I use (the Festo RO2E) is one of the very few on the market that, by means of a switch on the side, can be altered to be a conventional random orbital sander – which is good for fairly fine sanding, particularly on flat surfaces – or a fairly aggressive rotary sander. However, the thing that sets it apart is that the disc rotates in an eccentric orbit which more or less eliminates any circular scratch marks on the wood. I tend to use mine in this mode almost all the time.

Rotary sander

In appearance this is a similar machine to the RO2E but in use it is more like an angle grinder with an abrasive disc attached. The big difference between it and an angle grinder is that it has a built-in extraction system. With a 4in (102mm) disc, it's smaller than the RO2E but is much more aggressive. Attach a 40 grit disc to the velcro pad and it will remove the deep gouges made by the Arbortech very quickly indeed.

Belt sander

This sanding machine tends to gather dust beneath the bench in my workshop. For me it is too heavy and does not allow enough control to use for boxmaking.

Drills and saws

Power drill

Certainly my first power tool. When I started boxmaking I used it for just about everything. It gets less use now as purpose-made and fixed machines have replaced it but it hasn't yet gathered a coat of dust.

Drill bits

I tend to prefer lip-and-spur bits as these are far easier to position accurately than the more usual engineers' bit.

Circular saw

The dust does tend to remain undisturbed on this one. It has its uses of course but I certainly don't get it out much for boxmaking.

Jigsaw

This was the forerunner to my band saw. It is much cheaper than a band saw and much less hard work than a coping saw or bow saw. It's not really essential, but it's certainly time-saving.

Angle grinder

Many years ago I swapped a mirror frame which I had shaped (mostly using a foam drum sander) for a small angle grinder and it has influenced my work ever since. Fitted with an Arbortech, it's a formidable machine; it's also pretty formidable fitted with a coarse sanding disc (32 or 40 grit) but this does tend to fill the workshop with dust very quickly.

Fig 2.8 *Foam drum sander*

Fig 2.9 *The RO2E Festo random orbital/rotary sander*

Fig 2.10 *The Arbortech mounted on an angle grinder, rotary sander and random orbital/rotary sander*

Fig 2.11 *Rotary sander*

Fig 2.12 *The angle grinder with Arbortech attached*

STATIONARY MACHINES

Radial arm saw

This was my first machine. A table saw was out of the question due to lack of space. I wasn't doing very much ripping (for safety reasons I would never recommend ripping on a radial arm saw) and for short, boxmaking sizes I reckoned it would do the job. It's still going strong, though I think it's probably next in line for replacement and with more space now I will definitely invest in a table saw next time.

Router

I'm not sure whether this should come under fixed machines or hand-held machines. It's a hand-held really, but since I discovered the joys of using a router fixed under the table, it hardly ever emerges into the light. (See Jigs, p 16, for more information on my inverted router.)

Drill press

A pretty straightforward machine. This is a boon for drilling holes at right angles and I find I use it a lot for boxmaking. A floor-standing model, if it can be squeezed in, is well worth the extra cost.

Band saw

A very versatile saw. It will rip, crosscut to a limited length and, of course, cut curves.

Planer/thicknesser

I managed without a planing machine for years. I bought my wood planed, jointed the box, and used the Arbortech to take the box to its finished thickness. Since owning one I'm finding that I use it more and more. I'm probably just getting lazy. If I'm not careful my cherished hand plane might start to rust. I doubt it though: there's really nothing to beat the sound and feel of a thin shaving singing off a well-sharpened hand plane.

Shaper

When I started out on this book I had a router mounted under a table but time moves on and I now own a shaper. More widely found in US workshops than in the UK, I've come to really like mine. I'm not sure whether to describe it as a halfway stage between a router and a fully grown spindle shaper or some sort of cross between the two. It's probably both. A spindle shaper has always struck me as a rather heavy, somewhat dangerous machine, more suited to a large joinery workshop than one making small boxes. But I needed something more solid and accurate than my home-made router table (though it had served me long and well). A shaper seemed to fit the bill. Using the three-winged cutters on the 1in (25mm) spindle, it was easily tough enough for the small tenons and rabbets I was constantly needing and despite its relatively slow speeds (it has a choice of two: 8,000 or 10,000rpm), with a ¼in (6mm) collet mounted on the spindle, and using a straight router cutter, it seems quite happy to cut even a small groove.

Disc sander

My first stationary sanding machine, albeit a home-made one. By purchasing an aluminium disc and attaching it to a motor rescued from a petrol pump on a gas-station forecourt, I made my own disc sander, and I think I've got as good a machine as any available in the shops. In fact, it's a lot more solid than some manufactured disc sanders and it is this solidity which, for end grain, gives me good, accurate 90° or 45° angles. Dust extraction is achieved by attaching a hose to the box under the table. I suspect that dust extraction would improve a great deal if I extracted from all around the disc; I've got it on my things-to-do-list...

Fig 2.13 *Radial arm saw complete with its dust collection hood*

Fig 2.14 *Shaper – halfway between an inverted router and a fully grown spindle shaper*

Fig 2.15 *My home-made disc sander*

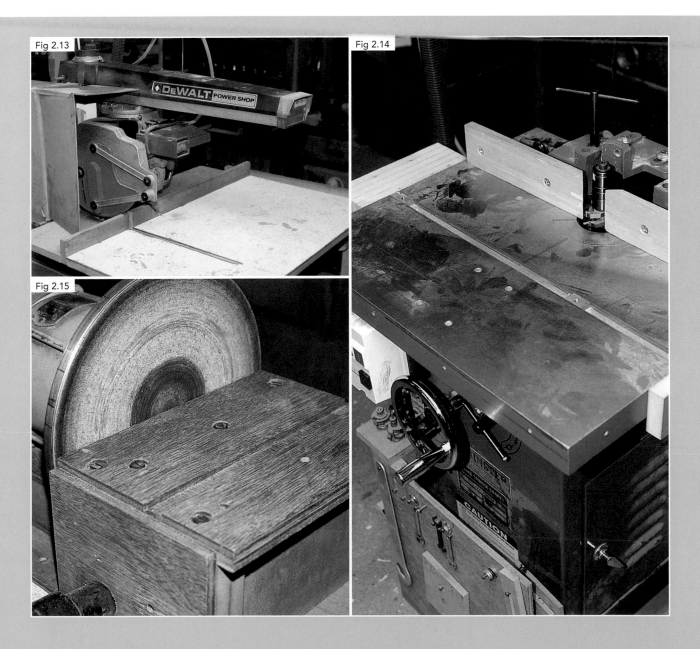

Fig 2.13

Fig 2.15

Fig 2.14

Belt linisher

This is one of my most recently acquired sanding machines and is a definite boon for sanding flat surfaces. Before I squeezed this machine into its new home I had two square boards of melamine-faced chipboard on both sides of which I had glued abrasive paper of various grits. When it came to levelling the bottom of a tray, I clamped the board into the vise and rubbed the tray back and forth on the sandpaper. In other words, my muscles were providing the power. Now, with a belt linisher, an electric motor does the hard work and I simply hold the tray, gently but firmly, on a moving belt. Be careful: this moving belt is quite capable of ripping a piece of wood out of your hand and hurling it across the workshop. It is also capable of turning the base of a tray into a cloud of dust in a matter of seconds.

JIGS

The sanding disc table

I'm not sure when a jig is not a jig and when it's a normal part of the machine, but I'll say a few words about this one here as it is home-made and I do use it quite a lot in other jigs.

Basically, it consists of an 18mm ($^3/_4$in) plywood box with a groove routed on the top to take a miter fence and various nuts set on the inside to allow other jigs to be bolted on. To fit these nuts, counter-bore a hole of a diameter equal to the distance across the flats of a hexagonal nut, and hammer them home. A hole at the bottom of the left-hand side of the box allows the connection of a hose for dust extraction. This would probably work better if I built a box all the way round the disc and extracted dust from around the whole of its circumference. I will do this. One day...

Hinge-making jigs

I use quite a few different jigs when I am making hinges. The first of these I use to cut the hinge piece to the correct length, plus 0.5mm ($^1/_{64}$in). It's hardly a jig at all really, but it did take a fair bit of head scratching before I came up with it. All it consists of is two pieces of waste wood of the same thickness – 18mm ($^3/_4$in) MDF is perfect – and a rod to pass through the hole in the hinge. It's a bit of a stretch calling it a jig but I thought it was a good wheeze for cutting the excess from the hinge pieces, using the hole as a reference. Since owning a table saw, I've found that the same thing can be done with a stop and a dowel inserted into the pivot hole (see Fig 2.21).

The next jig I use for making hinges is ... well I'm not really sure what to call it. How about an end-squaring-off-parallel-to-the-hole jig. It is a piece of plywood or MDF with two pieces of plywood glued onto the end of it. Two slots allow this to be bolted onto the sanding disc table. While the table saw is fairly accurate and produces a pretty

Fig 2.16 *A belt linisher gives your muscles a break*

Fig 2.17 *My sanding disc table*

Fig 2.18 *Construction of the sanding disc table*

Fig 2.19 *Cutting a hinge piece to length on the band saw, using the hole as a reference*

Fig 2.20 *Construction of the jig shown in Fig 2.19*

Fig 2.21 *Plan view of the jig shown in Fig 2.20*

Fig 2.22 *The end-squaring-off-parallel-to-the-hole jig*

Fig 2.23 *Sanding a hinge piece exactly to length*

Fig 2.24 *Sanding a large hinge piece to length*

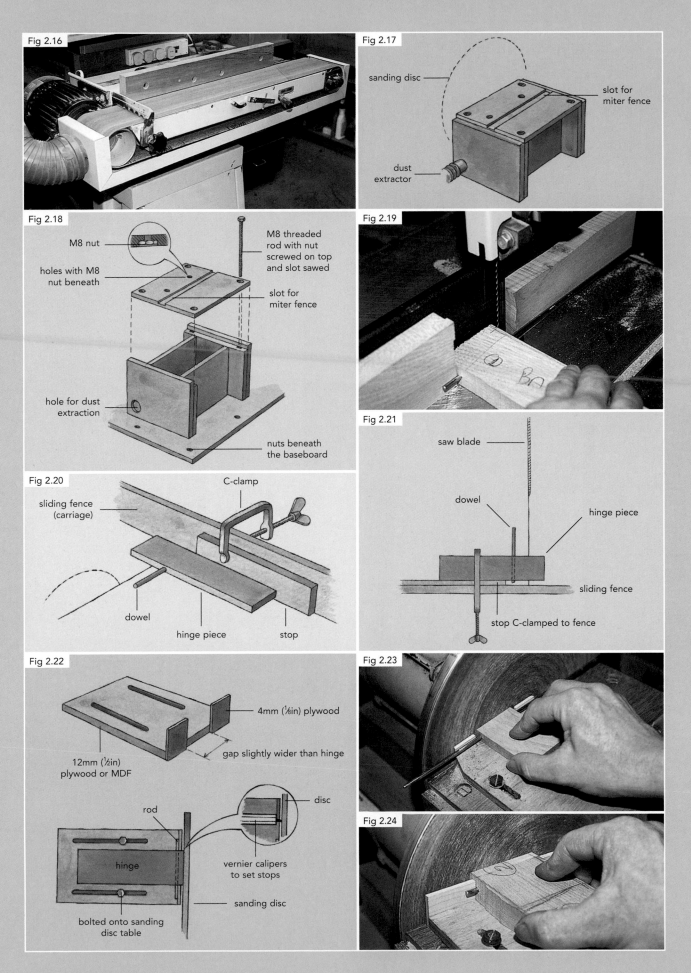

Fig 2.16

Fig 2.17

sanding disc

slot for
miter fence

dust
extractor

Fig 2.18

M8 nut

holes with M8
nut beneath

M8 threaded
rod with nut
screwed on top
and slot sawed

slot for
miter fence

hole for dust
extraction

nuts beneath
the baseboard

Fig 2.19

Fig 2.20

C-clamp

sliding fence
(carriage)

dowel

hinge piece

stop

Fig 2.21

saw blade

dowel

hinge piece

sliding fence

stop C-clamped to fence

Fig 2.22

4mm (⅛in) plywood

gap slightly wider than hinge

12mm (½in)
plywood or MDF

rod

disc

hinge

vernier calipers
to set stops

sanding disc

bolted onto sanding
disc table

Fig 2.23

Fig 2.24

good finish, the band saw certainly does not, and neither of them produces as good or as accurate a finish as this method. The distance from the stop, against which the rod rests, and the sanding disc needs to be set accurately, and I find the plunger end of my vernier calipers does this very well.

The next job in hinge making is the cutting of the knuckles. I use a jig for this too, which I have described fully for the work box and the jewelry box (see Chapters 9 and 11, pp 91 and 121).

Finally, on the jigs which relate specifically to hinges, there's the rounding-off jig. It's another bolt-on addition (see Figs 2.25 and 2.26).

Disc-making jig

Another bolt-on addition to the sanding disc. Again, hardly worthy of the name 'jig', this is used to smooth off a circle after it has been cut by saw or band saw. The center of the disc will need marking and drilling partway through with a 5mm ($^{13}/_{64}$in) drill bit. It simply consists of a swinging arm of 12mm ($^{1}/_{2}$in) plywood or MDF, large enough to support the size of disc being finished, with a counterbored hole in one end so that it can be pivoted to the sanding disc table, and a hole in the other end to take a short rod or peg that locates in the center of the required disc. I use an M8 bolt for the pivot and a 5mm ($^{13}/_{64}$in) dowel for the disc locater. The same setup can be used on the router or shaper.

Circle-cutting jig

To cut a circle which doesn't go all the way through (as for the jewelry box in Chapter 11, see p 130), an MDF plate bolted onto the bottom of the router base plate, with a hole for a pin, will do the job. The radius is measured from the center of the pin to the outside edge of the router cutter.

'T' jig

A 'T' jig consists of three pieces of MDF or plywood. Two of these are bolted onto the sanding disc and the third, cut to a 'T' shape, slides between them until the crosspiece butts up against them.

Tabletop

I know this is not really a jig but I must give a mention to my setting-out table. I needed somewhere to unroll the velvet and moiré, and while spreading it out on the office floor was just about alright, it certainly wasn't ideal. But I had no space for a 2m (6ft) table! There was a little room left on the ceiling, so I got hold of an old door (hollow interior, plywood-covered, flush-type), extended it a little (I wanted it about 1m [3ft] wide), covered it with some hardboard and suspended the whole lot from the ceiling. (At this point you must refer to the diagrams and photos: see Figs 2.32 and 2.33.)

Fig 2.25 *Rounding off the knuckles*

Fig 2.26 *Rounding off the knuckles of a large hinge*

Fig 2.27 *Sanding the edge of a disc*

Fig 2.28 *A pin inserted into an MDF box …*

Fig 2.29 *… locates in a hole in the center of the circle*

Fig 2.30 *The router removes a circle*

Fig 2.31 *The 'T' jig*

Fig 2.32 *The pulley mechanism of my tabletop*

I can't begin to explain how to make the pulleys work. At first I just hung the table from two simple pulleys but it was very heavy to pull up. What about a block and tackle? I thought I knew the principle.
I wanted it so that I could get it as high as possible, and raise and lower it while standing at the table, so the block and tackle had to operate horizontally. Could I get my brain to sort it out? I could not.
I puzzled and thought and sketched for hours. Literally. I think the gods finally took pity on me when they realized that I wasn't going to bed until I'd solved it.

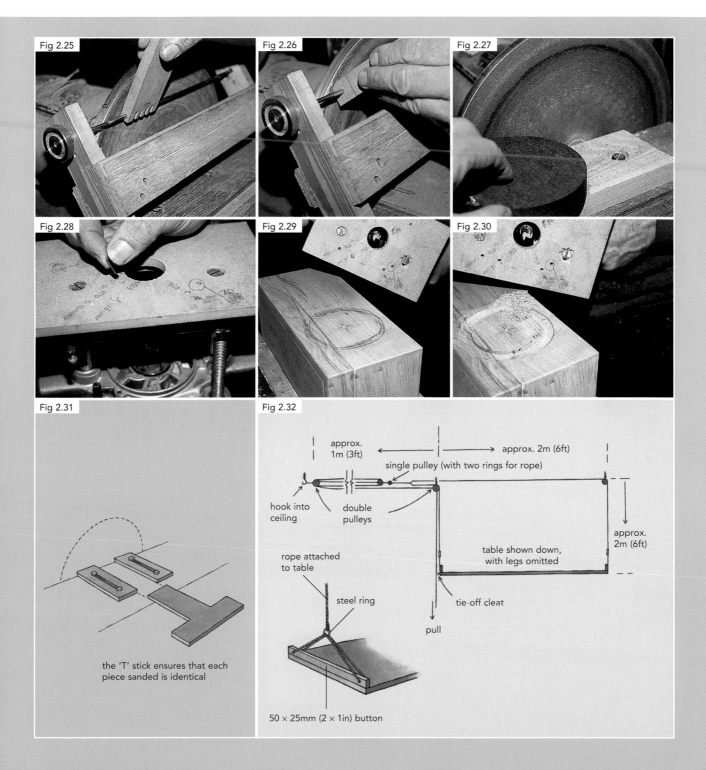

Fig 2.25

Fig 2.26

Fig 2.27

Fig 2.28

Fig 2.29

Fig 2.30

Fig 2.31

the 'T' stick ensures that each piece sanded is identical

Fig 2.32

approx. 1m (3ft)

approx. 2m (6ft)

single pulley (with two rings for rope)

hook into ceiling

double pulleys

rope attached to table

steel ring

table shown down, with legs omitted

approx. 2m (6ft)

tie-off cleat

pull

50 × 25mm (2 × 1in) button

Legs proved to be the next problem. In blissful naivety and ignorance, I reckoned that I could rest one side on two of my machines, and make two other legs to swing down. Well I could, and did, but it wobbled. Horribly. I very nearly gave up and consigned the whole lot to the stove. But in one final flash of inspiration I thought of clamping it to the machines. So, when I need to use the tabletop, I lower it and clamp it to the machines and when I've finished, I take the clamps off and raise it again. It's rock solid now and I'm very pleased with it.

Router fence

More than just a fence, this is a system which fulfills almost all my routing requirements. I've got it mounted on a shaper but I can see no reason why the same system can't be used on a router table.

The basic frame consists of two pieces of MDF bolted onto two more that run either side of the router table. (The router table must be absolutely parallel for this to work.) A piece of ash is screwed onto one of the crosspieces of MDF which acts as a fence. These cross-pieces can then slide back and forth to take the work at right angles across the cutter, or be fixed in position by the two Bristol locking levers that screw into nuts running in the 'T' groove.

There are two stops mounted on the router table that can be used either to limit the travel of the carriage or to 'remember' a setting for the fence. Additional stops to limit the length of travel can be clamped to the side runners as can various purpose-made jigs.

Having moved, halfway through this book, from an inverted router mounted under a board set on top of an old school desk, to a 'shaper', I find that for one project I use the old system for making a certain joint and for another I use the shaper for the same job. So, I'll write a few words on each.

My router used a fence which was pivoted with a bolt and wing nut at one end and a bolt and wing nut running in an arc at the other end. Or, to be more exact, running in one of two arcs. If I'd cut just one, the top would have had little strength left and the end would have fallen off. The other significant part of this system was the groove for the miter fence (see Fig 2.36).

The method I *now* use for cutting these joints is on the shaper, using my 'fence' system. The piece is clamped onto a sheet of MDF using two toggle clamps and the whole frame is slid forward, enabling a pair of three-winged cutters (separated with a spacer) to cut the tenon.

The manufacturers do recommend that the shaper not be used with cutters smaller than 30mm (1¼in) in diameter 'as the peripheral speed is inadequate to achieve a good finish on any cutter of 25mm (1in) or less'. I personally have not found this to be so. It certainly

Fig 2.33 *Securing the table in its 'up' position*

Fig 2.34 *The MDF 'fence' assembly which enables my shaper to do just about anything*

Fig 2.35 *The 'fence' on my shaper and the captive 'nut' which enables the frame to be slid back and forth or locked in position*

Fig 2.36 *Router table mark one. With its swinging arm fence, it did a sterling job for years*

Fig 2.37 *Shaper table with sliding fence/carriage*

Fig 2.38 *Cutting the tails with the Leigh jig*

Fig 2.39 *I use an electric drill, an ordinary twist bit and a 'spacer' or depth stop, through which the bit passes, to remove most of the waste: this eases the work of the dovetail cutter*

makes sense: a 3mm (⅛in) cutter turning at only 10,000rpm is definitely too slow but all I can say is, I use it with cutters down to this diameter and it seems to work. Maybe with softwood or less dense hardwoods I wouldn't get away with it...

Leigh dovetail jig

Way back, when I first started to make boxes, I used to hand-cut all the dovetails – they were very time-consuming and it wasn't long before I bought a Leigh dovetail jig. There are now many other dovetail jigs on the market, including the Woodrat, which enables

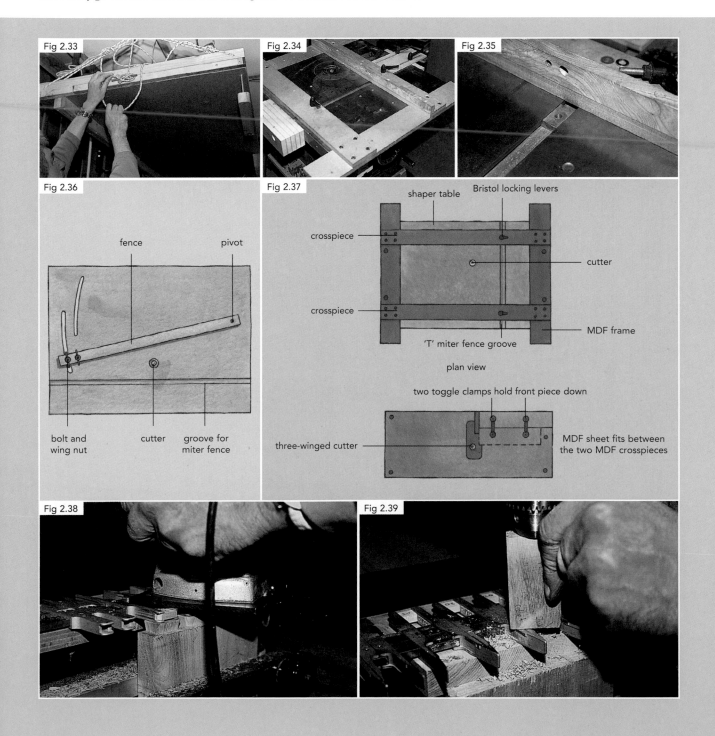

Fig 2.33

Fig 2.34

Fig 2.35

Fig 2.36

fence   pivot

bolt and   cutter   groove for
wing nut   miter fence

Fig 2.37

shaper table   Bristol locking levers

crosspiece

cutter

crosspiece

MDF frame

'T' miter fence groove

plan view

two toggle clamps hold front piece down

three-winged cutter

MDF sheet fits between
the two MDF crosspieces

Fig 2.38

Fig 2.39

you to space the dovetails as you wish. I used the Leigh for a long time but I have now moved on to a system, which I more or less dreamed up from scratch, that uses the sliding carriage on my shaper. I did find a couple of things when using the Leigh, one being that it must be accurately set, and the other that, when cutting the pins, drilling away some of the waste is a big help.

Spline cradle

This is a cradle to carry the square corner of a mitered box across a straight router cutter in order to cut a neat, square-bottomed groove. A spline can then be glued into this groove to make the box more attractive and interesting and, more importantly, to strengthen the joint.

Dowel cutter

I adapted this method of making dowels from a tip I came across in a woodworking magazine some years ago. This is one of the things I started doing when I was about halfway through writing this book. For the desk box (see Chapter 4, p 39), I describe making dowels by planing down a square section to an octagon and then tapering it. I stick by that! Wedging the joints with tapered pegs is an excellent way of securing them. However, since I hit upon this way of making dowels, I must admit that I tend to use these for my pegs now (see Fig 2.43).

Sanding block

Using offcuts of plywood and MDF, I made a very solid miter sanding block which bolts onto the sanding disc table. I find that this gives very good 45° angles.

Pieces of an old pool cue are very handy for wrapping sandpaper around to sand the inside of various radii.

SAFETY

Never rush, use guards and push sticks, wear eye protection; please work safely. I'm not going to list maxims and instructions: we all know them. The trouble is, they're so easy to forget or ignore 'just for this little job'. When a machine is working properly and being used properly it's like a pussycat in front of the fire. This is very deceptive. Rub its fur the wrong way and the pussycat can turn into a very powerful tiger.

A case in point. I wanted to reduce the thickness of a tiny piece of 4mm (1/8in) thick sycamore, and I wanted it reduced now. So I switched on the belt linisher and held the little piece of wood against the stop with my finger tip. The thickness reduced, the wood slipped under the stop and my finger suddenly found itself pressed hard onto a moving sanding belt. Ouch. I've now got a flattened finger tip; not too serious but totally unnecessary. Suppose I'd done something equally crazy on a circular saw.

Fig 2.40 *I found, when setting the Leigh jig, that the exact height of the cutter was very important*

Fig 2.41 *My 'cradle-for-making-spline-slots' jig*

Fig 2.42 *Gluing a triangle onto the 'cradle-for-making-spline-slots' jig*

Fig 2.43 *The dowel-making process*

Fig 2.44 *This miter block is bolted onto the sanding disc table*

Dust comes under the general heading of safety. When I started making boxes my only dust control was to open the shed door.
I graduated to a wall fan (not terribly efficient), then to a portable, wheeled vacuum cleaner (a considerable improvement). I now have a 2kW vacuum unit mounted on the wall with properly connected dust-extraction pipes running all round the ceiling. For the odd box, a weekend project, or when using hand tools, a big dust extraction unit is overkill. The dust extraction you need depends entirely on the type and quantity of work you're doing. At one end of the scale a disposable paper mask might be all that's needed. At the other end, a powered respirator and a fully plumbed-in system of dust and chip extraction might be the answer.

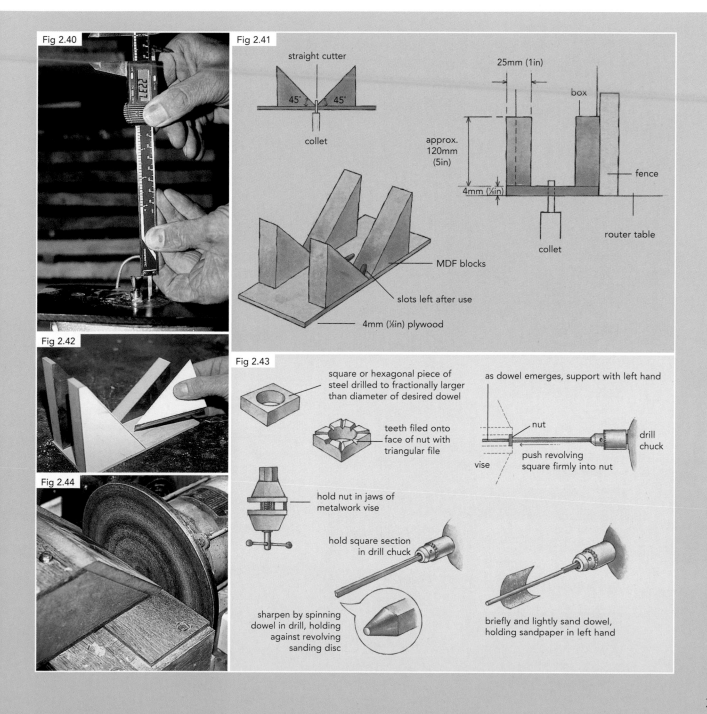

Fig 2.40

Fig 2.41
straight cutter
45°   45°
collet
25mm (1in)
box
approx.
120mm
(5in)
fence
4mm (⅙in)
collet
router table
MDF blocks
slots left after use
4mm (⅙in) plywood

Fig 2.42

Fig 2.43
square or hexagonal piece of steel drilled to fractionally larger than diameter of desired dowel
teeth filed onto face of nut with triangular file
hold nut in jaws of metalwork vise
hold square section in drill chuck
sharpen by spinning dowel in drill, holding against revolving sanding disc

as dowel emerges, support with left hand
nut
drill chuck
vise
push revolving square firmly into nut

briefly and lightly sand dowel, holding sandpaper in left hand

Fig 2.44

BASIC TECHNIQUES

Start with a project from this book by all means but use it as a springboard. Get a few of these techniques under your belt and then head off into your imagination. Boxes aren't limited to a base, a lid and four sides. There are so many possibilities for size, shape and material, I feel I haven't scratched the surface yet. There are still dozens of ideas jangling around inside my head – there just aren't enough hours in the day to make them all.

BOXES

MAPPING OUT

The first step in making a box is to map it out on your chosen plank – preferably a single plank. I like to use a single plank as the pieces can then be cut so that the figure runs right around the box. It also avoids the danger of any one piece looking out of place. It gives a feeling of 'oneness'.

The plank shown in the photos opposite was about 1500 × 210 × 17mm (5 × 8 × ¾in), and from this came a box of 300 × 200 × 70mm (12 × 8 × 2¾in); a well-proportioned box which I think is about right for a desktop. I don't want to get too bogged down with exact sizes though. Where they do matter, I'll mention them but generally speaking it's proportions that matter, not sizes – proportions of width, length and depth and the relationship between the thickness of the material to the size of the box. A box of 300 × 200mm (12 × 8in) seems to work fairly well up to around 140mm (5½in) in depth. If it needs to be deeper than this, I suggest an increase in size.

There is a 'golden rule' of proportion which states that, in a rectangle, the length should be 1.62 times the width. Applied to a box 200mm (8in) wide, the length would be 324mm (13in) which, come to think of it, are proportions that I have used from time to time...

Personally, I like a fairly chunky feel to boxes but even so, for a box of around 200 × 300mm (8 × 12in), I wouldn't make the sides much thicker than 16mm (⅝in). For a smaller box this could be reduced to about 14mm (⁹⁄₁₆in) while for a monster box, of something like 450 × 250mm (18 × 10in), the material could be around 18mm (¾in) thick.

When I say map out the box, I mean look at the plank – its grain, figure, color and shape – and decide which part of it would make the best lid and how the grain and patterns in the wood will eventually flow around the box. Is there an obvious handle along the waney edge or in the figure?

This plank was cupped a little, so I decided to make the lid for the eventual box convex. I try to work with the wood, try to let the wood itself decide what sort of box it will become.

Now is the time to choose which side of the plank will be the outside of the box. Don't forget to look carefully at both sides. I have to admit that more than once I've mapped out a beautiful box on a piece of wood only to turn it over and find a large knot or some other defect right on a joint. It's always best to find these things out before cutting. Maybe I'll learn someday.

CONSTRUCTION

I shall go into the construction of a box in some detail in Chapter 4 (see p 39). Then, when I'm describing variations for the other boxes, you can refer back to those construction details and I can concentrate on what gives each box its individual character.

FINISHES

I finish almost all of my boxes with two or three coats of Danish oil followed by a coat of beeswax. The wax I use is in emulsion; it is mixed with a solvent which evaporates from the surface of the wood to leave a coating of wax behind. In the jar it has the consistency of thick-set yogurt. I apply it with a wad of 0000 steel wool, which denibs the surface, getting rid of any lumps and bumps of dust particles which have set themselves in the surface of the oil. I then finish it off with a soft cotton cloth. Old T-shirts are my personal preference.

For oak I make an exception. Steel wool and oak do not go very well together. Tiny particles of steel wool can lodge in the grain and, in time, react with the tannin in the oak to stain it black. For oak I use a plastic scourer or a cloth to apply the wax.

Fig 3.1 *Starting to map out. Each piece is numbered so that, once they are sawn, you don't spend ages trying to find out which should be joined to which*

Fig 3.2 *The lid is marked onto the plank – with plenty to spare*

Fig 3.1

Fig 3.2

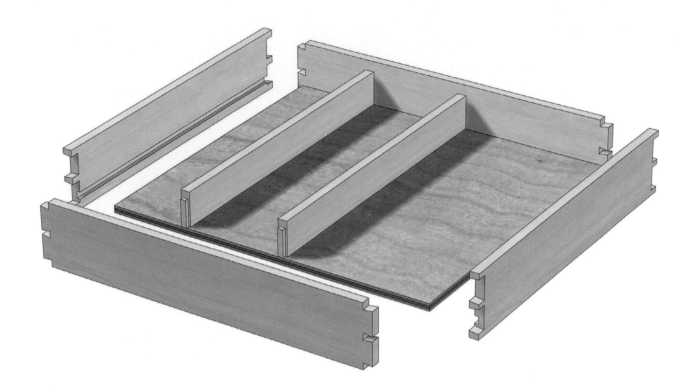

TRAYS

Maybe I'm a glutton for punishment or maybe I just choose the most difficult way of doing things but I always dovetail the trays in my boxes. I just like the way they hold together without a drop of glue in sight. They could be mitered and then reinforced with splines and I'm sure they'd stay together for centuries. Without splines I'm not so sure – failed miters tend to be one of the problems with antique boxes. And I think glue should keep rather than hold pieces of wood together. There is a difference; in *holding* the glue does all the work while in *keeping* the joint does the holding and the glue just secures it. That's why I use dovetails. They're not that difficult and I really think they are worth it.

There are lots of different ways of making trays; this is just the way I make them.

THE WOOD

First things first. Ripple sycamore is almost always my first choice. It is attractive, close-grained, and goes with almost any other wood. I emphasize *almost* any other wood: I find it doesn't go with woods that are too close in color, such as other sycamores, silver birch or a light beech. I have used a red beech for trays but I found the grain a bit difficult for cutting the fine dovetails required. I intend to try some American black walnut, though I've got a feeling that I'm going to find the contrast a bit too severe, so I shall probably switch to English walnut.

THE PROCESS

The trays shown here are made from 5mm ($^{13}/_{64}$in) wood and are 35mm (1$^3/_8$in) wide. Take the dimensions for your tray from your box, not with a ruler but by marking the wood for the tray. For the sides of the trays, I hold the wood against the side of the box and mark it off. For the fronts and backs of the trays, assuming there are two layers, I usually make one tray just larger than square for the top layer and cut the second tray to make up the difference. For the bottom layer, I make the two trays equal. For a tray 200 × 180mm (8 × 7in), start with a piece at least 800mm (32in) in length and something over 36mm (1$^{13}/_{32}$in) in width. Plane it down to 36mm (1$^{13}/_{32}$in), then take off 6mm ($^1/_4$in) slices. A band saw is less wasteful than a circular saw but a circular saw with a good ripping blade is faster and stays sharp for considerably longer. Put these slices through a drum sander to take them to 5mm ($^{13}/_{64}$in) They could be thicknessed by machine or planed by hand but razor-sharp blades are essential if you're dealing with ripple sycamore. If you plane this with less-than-sharp blades, the fibers of the wood will catch and break and your gorgeous sycamore will be left with deep scars in its surface. Walnut would be far more biddable. For this job, it's the availability of machines that will influence your choice of material. Alternatively, you could ask your wood supplier to deep cut (that is, cut through the thickness) a 25mm (1in) board and then get either them or a large joinery shop to machine-sand it to 5mm ($^{13}/_{64}$in). These 5mm ($^{13}/_{64}$in) pieces could then be cut into 35mm(1$^3/_8$in) strips.

Fig 3.3 *Sycamore cut to 37mm (1$^7/_{16}$in) wide, ready to be cut into 5mm ($^3/_{64}$) strips*

Fig 3.4 *Using a circular saw for this was a bit wasteful – too much of the beautiful wood was reduced to sawdust for my liking – but much faster than a band saw*

Fig 3.3

Fig 3.4

Sides, front and back

For each tray, mark a strip into four lengths, roughly 20mm (³⁄₄in) over what is required, for the sides (the length pieces), and the front and back (the width pieces), and number them so that you can use them in the same order once they have been cut. This will ensure that the figure follows its natural pattern and appears to match, all the way around. For this reason, remember to mark on the lengths alternating the sides with the front and back. Cut the strip into the four pieces and square off one end of each piece, either on a shooting board or with the disc sander. Offer the front or back piece up to the width of the box and mark on the exact length required, with a pencil, on the unsquared end. Transfer this mark to the other width piece. Now square these ends to the pencil marks. If there are to be two trays side by side, square both ends of the width pieces for one tray, then follow the process above for the second tray. I keep the box next to the disc sander so that I can constantly check the fit. The trays need to be a good fit so that they are tight without being forced. Cut the sides for each tray in the same way.

Dovetails

Now for those dovetails. Set up the router with an arbor and mount two slotting cutters with spacers between them. For one of the spacers, I use a steel disc the radius of which is 5.5mm less than the radius of the slotting cutters. This acts as a depth stop. It is unlikely that you will be able to buy a disc like this, so unless you have a metalworking lathe you will need to find an engineer to turn down a mild steel bar to the correct diameter, drill it for the arbor, and then pare off a thin slice. (Mine is 1.25mm (³⁄₆₄in) thick.)

Clamp the width pieces for all your trays together, using waste wood at both ends, and pass them through these cutters, preferably using a miter fence, until the depth disc rubs against the end grain. You will now have three perfectly cut square pins. Cut the tailpieces in exactly the same way by rearranging the spacers and cutters.

The depth disc does burn slightly but as long as you don't keep up the pressure, the mark will be insignificant and can be removed later.

Next, pare the tails down gently to a dovetail shape, with a sharp chisel – I think a slope of 1:8 looks about right – and trim the tails square at the shoulder line.

Now, with the pin piece in the vise protruding about 10mm (³⁄₈in), position the correct tailpiece over the pin. Using a propelling pencil, preferably 0.5mm and with a hard lead, mark the shape of the slopes onto the pins, then pare these vertically to fractionally inside the pencil line.

With all four joints made, hold the frame in the vise and very carefully – it's a little bit fragile at this stage – plane the bottom edge so that it is flat all round.

Fig 3.5 *Two trays, numbered to indicate which end should be joined to which, and identified by a letter so that the pieces don't get muddled up*

Fig 3.6 *The tray pieces sandwiched between two pieces of MDF*

Fig 3.7 *Pins cut square*

Fig 3.8 *Paring down the tails with a sharp chisel*

Fig 3.9 *Paring down the tails – a different view*

Fig 3.10 *Removing waste from between the tails*

Fig 3.11 *Paring the pins to the pencil line*

Fig 3.12 *Ensuring there are no steps*

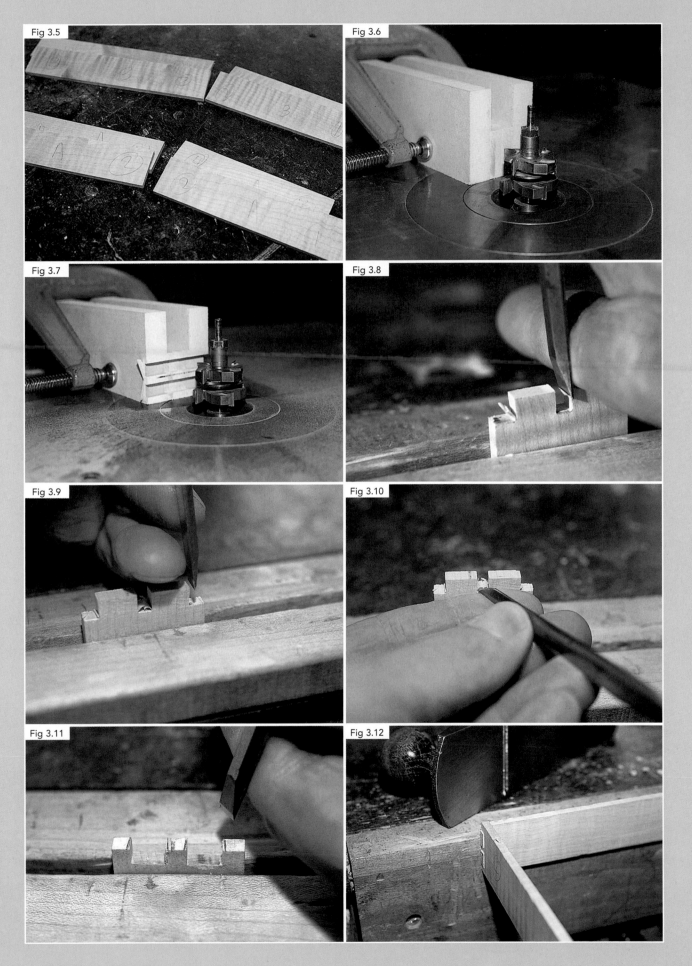

Fig 3.5

Fig 3.6

Fig 3.7

Fig 3.8

Fig 3.9

Fig 3.10

Fig 3.11

Fig 3.12

Set the router up with a 4mm ($^5/_{32}$in) straight cutter and, with the fence set at 6.5mm ($^1/_4$in), rout a groove in the pin pieces 2.5mm ($^7/_{64}$in) deep. This should be fractionally above the bottom of the pin and therefore doesn't need to be stopped. However, the grooves on the dovetailed pieces, also 2.5mm ($^7/_{64}$in) deep, must be stopped, and it's a good idea to set stops on the router rather than rely on a pencil mark. Square off the ends of the stopped grooves with a chisel.

Internal pieces

Reassemble the frame, measure the internal dimensions, add 4.5mm ($^5/_{32}$in) all round, and cut a 4mm ($^3/_{32}$in), birch-faced piece of plywood to this size, for the base.

Using PVA glue as thin as possible – so that it dries almost instantly – stick a piece of moiré to the underside of the plywood. Moiré is any fabric with a wave-like appearance. It is sometimes silk, but is more often a man-made fabric. Double-sided tape is an alternative to glue, or you could simply sand the underside of the plywood to a fine finish.

For the crosspieces that will divide the trays, use a 3mm ($^7/_{64}$in) straight cutter in the router, set stops and use a miter fence.

Cut the dividers to the inside dimension plus 4.5mm ($^5/_{32}$in), then cut tiny shoulders using two slotting cutters on an arbor, and finish the top of the shoulders by hand.

Assemble the tray dry to make sure everything fits. If the base doesn't fit into the groove, plane a very shallow chamfer on the top edge. If all is well, sand all the inside faces to 400 grit and oil the 6.5mm ($^1/_4$in) inside face beneath the groove. If you don't oil it at this stage it's very difficult to keep the oil off the moiré once the whole thing is finished.

Using a thin paintbrush, dab PVA glue onto the joints, leaving the inside third clean: you don't want glue squeezing out into the corner of the tray if you can help it. Using the nozzle of the glue tube, squirt a thin bead of glue into the grooves, then assemble the tray, clamping the dovetails with four little brass sash clamps. I find these perfect for providing pressure exactly where it's needed.

Before putting it to one side to dry, check for square using a rule or squaring rod. It's also a good idea to check that it's not twisted, either by using a flat surface or by sighting across it.

Once the glue has hardened, trim the tails and pins flat with a chisel and sand the whole thing to 400 grit.

Velvet lining

Velvet can be bought in many different qualities. Broadly, there are upholstery, curtain and dressmaking velvets. I tend to prefer dressmaking velvet in rich dark colors.

Latex glue, which I use a lot for gluing velvet, is wonderful stuff. When spread onto one surface, it acts like a normal adhesive and

Fig 3.13 *Routing a groove to take the base*

Fig 3.14 *Squaring the end of the tail-piece groove*

Fig 3.15 *Cutting the groove for the crosspiece; the carriage, or frame, slides forward with the tray piece held against a stop*

Fig 3.16 *Carefully removing the tray piece*

Fig 3.17 *Cutting the shoulders using slotting cutters*

Fig 3.18 *Finishing the shoulder 'top'*

Fig 3.19 *All the bits ready to go*

Fig 3.20 *Clamping up using Japanese miniature bar clamps*

Fig 3.21 *Using the squaring rod to check for square; I know the base was made perfectly square but there was 0.5mm ($^1/_{64}$in) extra all round so it could be slightly out*

Fig 3.22 *Once the glue has hardened, trim the dovetails flat with a sharp chisel*

Fig 3.23 *My cork block has a very slight convex curve sanded onto it; this helps to keep the tray side flat when you're sanding it*

Fig 3.24 *Measuring the tray using a zero-ended rule*

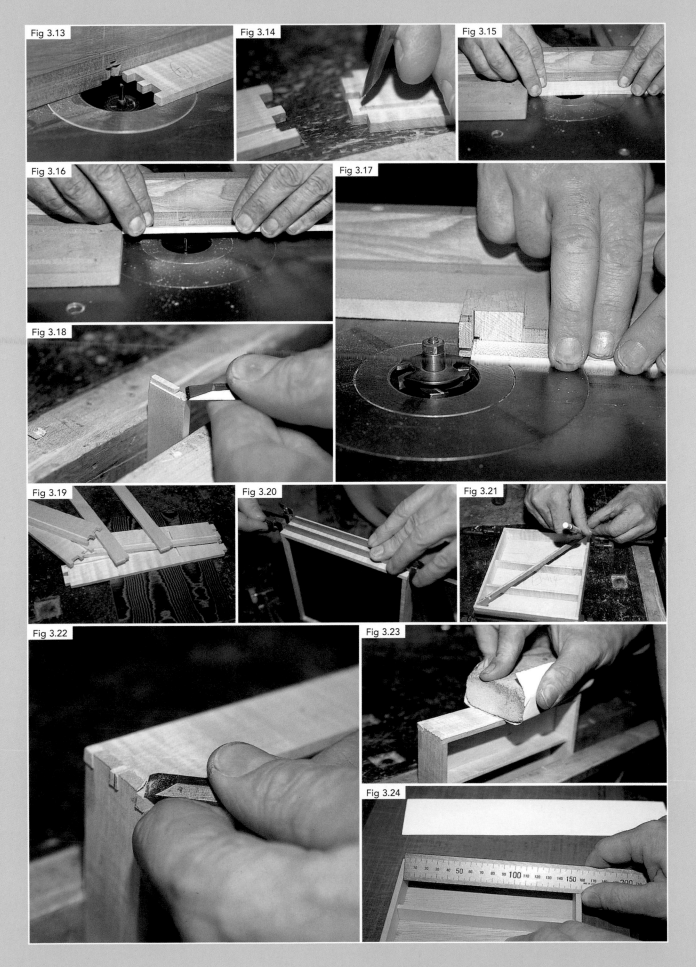

Fig 3.13

Fig 3.14

Fig 3.15

Fig 3.16

Fig 3.17

Fig 3.18

Fig 3.19

Fig 3.20

Fig 3.21

Fig 3.22

Fig 3.23

Fig 3.24

works very well with fabrics and leather. Spread onto both surfaces and allowed to dry, it works like a contact adhesive.

Cut a piece of card 1.5mm ($^1/_{16}$in) smaller than the inside of the compartment. With a few minute drops of latex glue, stick this card to the back of the velvet – more than just a hint of glue will bleed through to the surface of the velvet. Number the pieces of card and make sure that the pile of the velvet lies in the same direction on each piece. Velvet can look a totally different color depending on whether the light falls with or against the pile.

Using a craft knife or a pair of scissors, cut the velvet around the card, leaving a border of about 15mm ($^5/_8$in). Cut the corners from the velvet, about 1mm ($^1/_{16}$in) away from the corners of the card, so that when it is folded underneath, the card doesn't show. Glue the tabs to the underside of the card. Stick the panels into the tray with a few blobs of glue, again making sure that the direction of the pile on each strip is facing the same way.

Ring holders

You should allow 13mm ($^1/_2$in) between divisions for each ring holder, assuming that the foam to be used is 11mm ($^3/_8$in) thick. So, to include four ring holders in one division, it will need to be 52mm (2in) wide.

For this tray I cut a piece of 1.5mm ($^1/_{16}$in) plywood, 18mm ($^3/_4$in) wide and 3mm ($^7/_{64}$in) shorter than the width of the compartment. Assuming a tray depth of 35mm ($1^3/_8$in), these pieces of plywood should always be 18mm ($^3/_4$in) wide and 3mm ($^7/_{64}$in) shorter than the space they're to fit into. Slightly round the top corners, using a

scrap of sandpaper. Glue this onto a piece of 11mm ($^3/_8$in) foam cut to a 43mm ($1^{11}/_{16}$in) strip, then roll the plywood in order to cover it with the foam. (If you spread the latex glue onto both plywood and foam and let it dry, it will work as a contact adhesive and stick almost instantly.) Trim the foam to the same length as the plywood.

Cut a 54mm ($2^1/_8$in) strip of velvet about 30mm ($1^1/_4$in) longer than the plywood and glue this to the bottom edge of the foam. Roll the velvet tightly around the foam and glue the other edge down.

Make two cuts about 5mm ($^{13}/_{64}$in) either side of the top of the velvet. This will leave three flaps. Glue each of these down in turn, finishing with the top flap. Trim off any whiskery bits, pop the holder into the tray and move onto the next one. A blob of latex glue on the base of the tray will keep them in place.

Fig 3.25 *Leave a border of about 15mm (⅝in) when you cut the velvet*

Fig 3.26 *Cutting corners – use two cuts rather than one straight cut*

Fig 3.27 *Folding and sticking the velvet to the underside of the card*

Fig 3.28 *Pushing in the corners with a paper knife; a pointed stick would do just as well*

Fig 3.29 *Gluing the 1.5mm (⅛in) plywood onto the foam*

Fig 3.30 *Brush the glue onto both surfaces and allow it to dry before sticking the velvet down*

Fig 3.31 *Hold the foam down for a few minutes or it will spring back*

Fig 3.32 *Gluing the velvet to the bottom of the foam*

Fig 3.33 *Roll the velvet over the foam and then glue the free end underneath*

Fig 3.34 *Cut three tabs on the ends*

Fig 3.35 *Stick the side tabs down first, then the top*

Fig 3.36 *The velvet-covered inserts should be a snug fit in the tray*

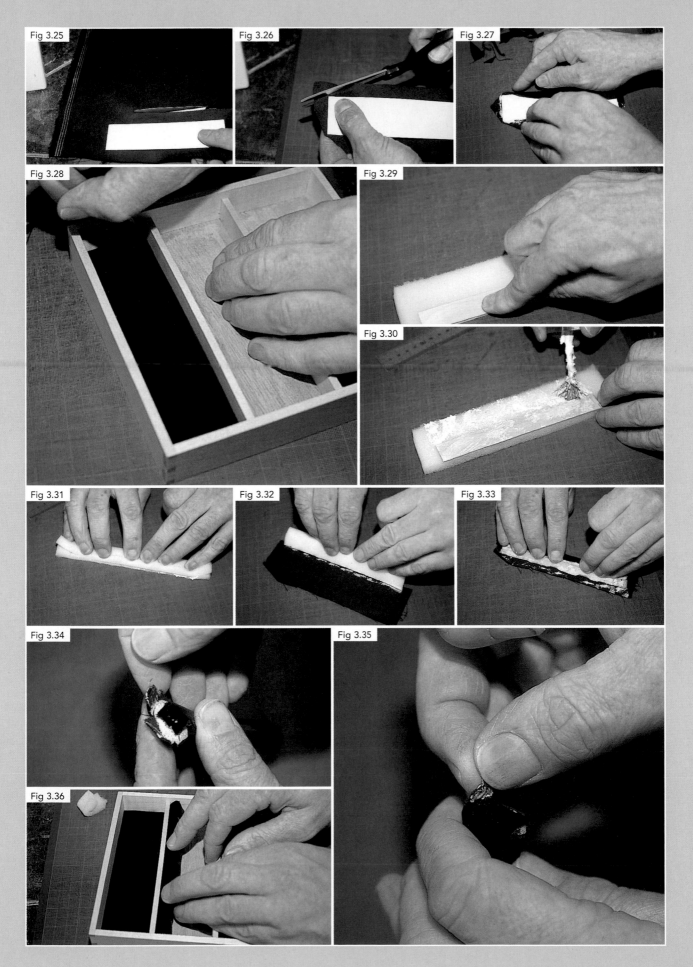

Fig 3.25

Fig 3.26

Fig 3.27

Fig 3.28

Fig 3.29

Fig 3.30

Fig 3.31

Fig 3.32

Fig 3.33

Fig 3.34

Fig 3.35

Fig 3.36

PIVOT HINGE

A bit of a silly name really as all hinges are pivot hinges – they wouldn't
work otherwise. I think that these came to be known as pivot hinges
because the pivot was the hinge. It's a hinge without the hinge part or,
to put it another way, for these boxes, the lid is the hinge. These hinges
have two advantages. The first is that the wood can move more or less
wherever it wants and the hinge will still work; any movement in the width
of the lid won't affect its operation. The second is that the material for the
lid can be shaped in any way. The Arbortech can do its worst;
as long as the pivots are in line, the hinge will work.

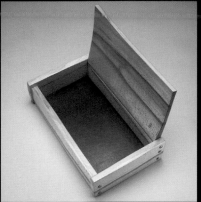

Desk box

p 39

Tilt hinge box

p 47

Mitered finger-hole box

p 55

Cash box

p 63

Writing slope

p 75

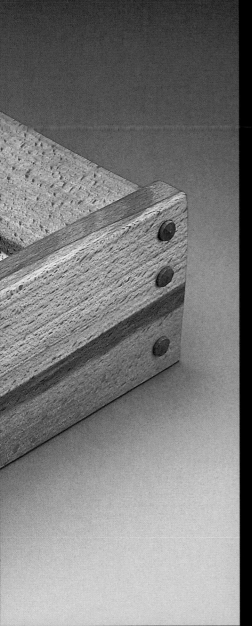

W ooden pegs form the hinge for this desk box which, with a little stretching of sizes and/or the addition of trays, can be transformed into innumerable different designs.

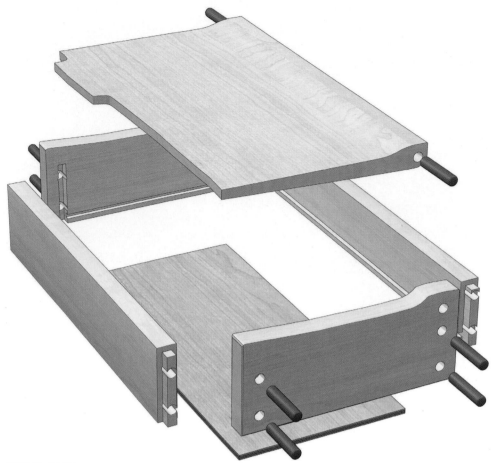

THE WOOD

I generally don't like beech. I always associate it with school desks, usually covered in graffiti, but otherwise fairly plain in figure and texture. However, as with most woods, there are always exceptions to the rule – the beech I used for this box had vivid red streaks.

THE PROCESS

Down to the nitty gritty. Having mapped out your box as described in Chapter 3, plane a straight edge and cut the pieces square and equal. The sides in particular must be square: if they're not, the joints won't be parallel and the box won't come together. For the same reasons, the back and front must be parallel.

The carcass

Cut the back so that its width is about 8mm (⁵⁄₁₆in) less than the width of the front. This will allow the lid to be thinner at the front than the back and not slope down. Don't worry about thickness and smoothness yet. The pieces do need to be flat, at least on one side, but not necessarily smooth.

At this stage it won't hurt to set the pieces out on the bench just to check that everything is in order and looks good. I find that it is very easy to get the left and right sides confused and make mistakes. With an 8mm (⁵⁄₁₆in) cutter in an inverted router, cut two grooves in each side piece, stopping them about 10mm (³⁄₈in) from the top of the front and back. Don't forget that the front and back are different sizes so the groove will finish lower at the back. The center of the cutter to the fence should be about 16mm (⁵⁄₈in).

It's debatable whether to take the whole depth – about 8mm (⁵⁄₁₆in) – in one cut or to take two passes. As a rule of thumb, a cutter should be happy cutting its own diameter in one pass so, in theory, one cut should be fine but I tend to use two: that way I'm not straining the machine or the cutter.

Don't worry too much about tear-out – it's bound to happen and it's best just to let it and plane it off later.

Set the pieces up on the bench and check that everything is still looking good. Scribble a circle on the outside of both ends to indicate the position of the hole for the hinge pivot.

Now set up the router with an arbor and two slotting cutters (see Figs 4.4 and 4.5), and use a wooden stop to set the depth of cut to about 8mm (⁵⁄₁₆in). (See Chapter 2, p 21, Figs 2.36 and 2.37.) With the wood held firmly against the miter fence cut a test tenon, using several passes, and check that it has a good snug fit: too loose a fit and the glue won't work, too tight a fit and you risk splitting the end piece. Once you're happy with the fit you can cut the tenons on the sides. If the edges weren't parallel, working from both edges, the joints at the ends will be seriously out, so do check them very carefully.

Fig 4.1 *Pieces of the box cut square and to equal length*

Fig 4.2 *Just to reassure yourself that all's well, stand the pieces on the bench*

Fig 4.3 *Routing the groove for the tenons on the front and back pieces*

Fig 4.4 *Slotting cutters mounted on an arbor*

Fig 4.5 *The wooden stop 'sets' the piece at the correct distance from the cutters. Take several cuts before using the stop to take the final skim*

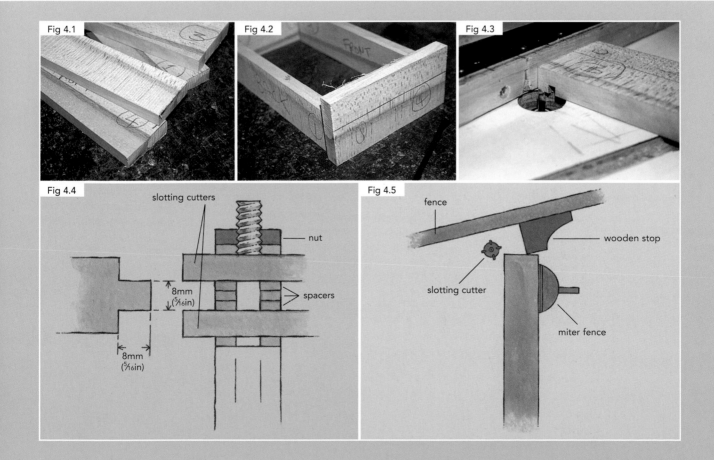

Fig 4.1

Fig 4.2

Fig 4.3

Fig 4.4

slotting cutters
nut
8mm (⁵⁄₁₆in)
spacers
8mm (⁵⁄₁₆in)

Fig 4.5

fence
wooden stop
slotting cutter
miter fence

Be gentle with the router. Using it like this puts a serious strain on it and only a medium or large router will do. Again, don't worry too much about tear-outs – they can be dealt with later.

Set the pieces up on the bench and mark the position of the top of the housing on the tenon, subtracting a couple of millimeters (about $5/64$in) to avoid any chance of it stopping before the bottoms are lined up. Next, cut off the shoulder, finishing it exactly flush with a chisel.

Now you can deal with those tear-outs by planing the bottoms and tops of the front and back and the bottoms of the ends. Measure the front and back. Make sure they're still parallel and that the front is still about 8mm ($5/16$in) wider than the back.

Fit the pieces back together, this time on a flat surface, and check that the carcass doesn't rock. If it does, plane it until it sits firm and happy. Measure for the base, about $5^1/2$mm ($1/4$in) oversize all round.

Now it is back to the router to cut the groove for the base. A 5mm ($13/64$in) cutter is about right for 4mm ($5/32$in) plywood plus leather. Rout a groove 6mm ($1/4$in) deep, about 6mm ($1/4$in) up from the bottom. This can be done comfortably in two passes. The leather I use for lining my boxes is generally about 1mm ($1/32$in) thick. If yours is slightly thicker or thinner then it's important that you cut the groove accordingly or, alternatively, plane the plywood edges slightly.

Cut the plywood base and check for fit; it should have about 1mm ($1/32$in) of movement. Sand one side then cover the other with leather. I use a special PVA that is made for leather but wood PVA, slightly watered-down, would do. The traditional adhesive for this is a heavy-duty wallpaper paste. If the base is a tight fit in the groove, hammer the edge, with the plywood supported on a firm, flat base, to reduce the thickness of the leather.

With all the pieces assembled, mark the position of the hinge pivot (see Fig 4.10), then drill an 8.5mm ($11/32$in) hole.

Now sand the front and back, inside and out, and the sides, inside only. If the wood is fairly thick I generally use an Arbortech to put a slight curve on the outside of the front and back, before the sanding.

Check the joints to ensure that the shoulder is tight up against the side and that the tenon is about 0.5mm ($1/64$in) short in the housing.

As always, assemble and clamp the box dry before gluing up. Things go wrong when you're gluing up; they even go wrong when you have done a dummy run but at least doing a dry run enables you to realize that the clamps you thought would do won't as the pieces that fitted perfectly when they were alone completely refuse to fit when the whole thing is assembled.

Take the phone off the hook and glue the box up. Have the clamps ready. Do not use too much glue. Blocks are not necessary as the ends have not been finished yet. Check for square using a squaring rod across the diagonals. If it's out, tilt the clamps slightly.

Fig 4.6 *The stop in action*

Fig 4.7 *Removing the tenon 'top'*

Fig 4.8 *Measuring the base and adding 11mm ($7/16$in)*

Fig 4.9 *Cutting the groove for the base; it runs through on the front and back but is stopped on the sides, at the grooves*

Fig 4.10 *Positioning the hinge pivot hole*

Fig 4.11 *Sanding the front and back to a slightly concave shape gives the whole box a softer, more natural feel and makes the pieces appear thinner*

Fig 4.12 *There shouldn't really be a gap here at all, but I'd much rather it was here than somewhere visible – it's insurance*

Fig 4.13 *My old wooden sash clamps; they are semi-retired now but they can still do the job*

Fig 4.14 *Hopefully clamp tilting will not be necessary*

Fig 4.15 *Lining the back of the box up with the pivot holes*

Fig 4.16 *Plane the back of the lid until it is perfectly in line with the pivot holes*

Fig 4.17 *With the lid in the machine vise, make sure the back of the lid lines up with the drill bit*

The lid

Now cut the lid to fit exactly between the sides. A tight fit is what you're aiming for at this stage. Plane the back of the lid until it just tips the two pivot holes; plane it, pop it on, check it, take it off, plane it again, pop it on, and so on until done.

Using a marking gauge, mark the position of the pivot holes on the sides of the lid. Set the box up in a machine vise, check that the drill bit is parallel to the edge of the lid and, with an 8mm (⁵⁄₁₆in) bit, drill to a depth of about 30mm (1¼in).

To make the pegs, plane a length of 8.5mm (¹¹⁄₃₂in) square-section material to an octagon, place it flat on the bench, then plane it to a round

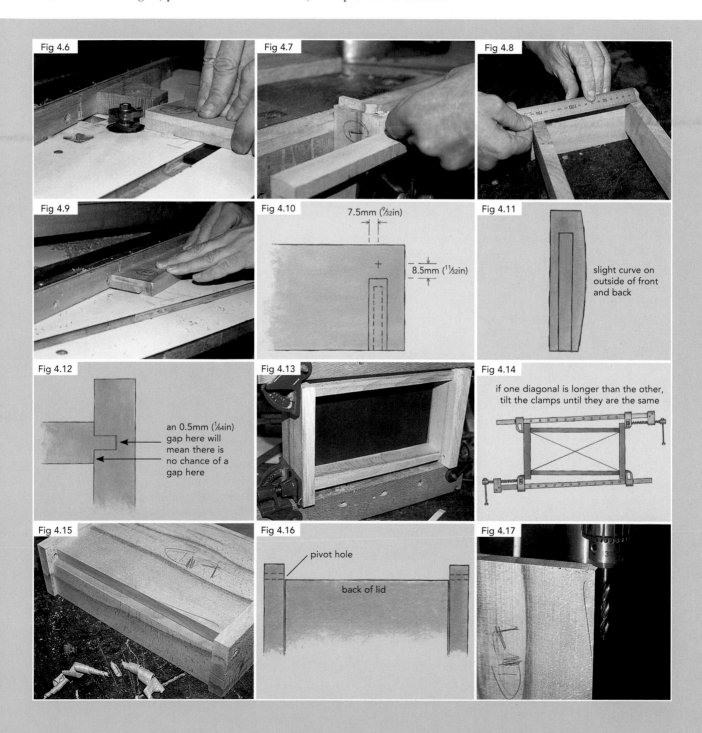

Fig 4.6

Fig 4.7

Fig 4.8

Fig 4.9

Fig 4.10
7.5mm (⁹⁄₃₂in)
8.5mm (¹¹⁄₃₂in)

Fig 4.11
slight curve on outside of front and back

Fig 4.12
an 0.5mm (¹⁄₆₄in) gap here will mean there is no chance of a gap here

Fig 4.13

Fig 4.14
if one diagonal is longer than the other, tilt the clamps until they are the same

Fig 4.15

Fig 4.16
pivot hole
back of lid

Fig 4.17

with a slight taper. I sometimes use a contrasting wood for the pegs but more often than not I use the same wood as the rest of the box: as it is end grain, this provides a sufficient contrast anyway.

Plane a quarter-round on the bottom edge of the back of the lid, pop the pegs in and check for rotation. This usually takes several puttings-on and takings-off but it's worth doing carefully. There should be about 1mm (^{1}/$_{32}$in) clearance under the lid.

Now decide on the shape for the lid. The figure on the ends might suggest a concave or convex shape. With this box, the slight cupping of the lid suggested a convex curve. Starting with the Arbortech, then using a surform and finally sanding, I carved the underside and top of the lid to a tapered convex shape. Looking at the figure in the lid more closely, I considered a plain, straight lip for the handle but on reflection I thought a sweeping curve might look better. Set the lid to one side.

Final shaping

Shape the sides of the box in the same way as the front and back, using the Arbortech. Next, mark out and drill 8mm (^{5}/$_{16}$in) holes for reinforcing pegs. The idea of these pegs, in addition to being decorative, is to make the joint a little like a wedged tenon. It's a good idea to drill these holes before sanding the sides as any slight slips with the drill can then easily be removed. Now sand the sides and the lid to 400 grit. Sand the top edge of the sides, leaving a slight lip above the lid, then sand the bottom edge, checking that the box doesn't rock on a flat surface.

The pegs

Cut eight pegs in the same way as the lid pivots but with a little more of a taper. The exact amount of taper tends to be a compromise between a good, tight-fitting peg and splitting the wood. Two or three taps with a hammer should be enough to knock it to the bottom of the hole. Leave the pegs well over-length and, dropping a little glue right into the bottom of the hole, tap them home. At this stage it is definitely not a good thing to have glue being forced out around the pegs and onto the finely sanded wood, so be sparing in its application. Cut the pegs off to about 4mm (^{5}/$_{32}$in), using a dovetail saw. As you reach the bottom of the cut, take care that the last piece doesn't split away. Finally, using a chisel bevel-side down, cut four facets onto the ends.

Finishing

Resist the urge to fix the lid on. It is far easier to finish the box and lid separately, and then fix the lid in place. I gave this box two coats of Danish oil and a finish with beeswax before fixing on the lid with its two hinge pivots. These should be finished off in the same way as the pegs, only this time it's a good idea to have a piece of cloth or something soft in the vise to avoid damaging the finished box. Rub a dab of oil on the raw hinge pivot and the box is complete.

Fig 4.18 *Planing the wood to shape for the pegs*

Fig 4.19 *The underside, back edge of the lid must be rounded off to allow clean movement of the lid*

Fig 4.20 *The underside, back edge of the lid, rounded off*

Fig 4.21 *Checking for clearance between the lid and back*

Fig 4.22 *The edge of the lid showing roughly the finished shape*

Fig 4.23 *The lid tapers to about 8mm (^{5}/$_{16}$in) at the front*

Fig 4.24 *Starting to shape the lid, with the Arbortech*

Fig 4.25 *A piece of masking tape around the drill bit will ensure that all the holes are the same depth*

Fig 4.26 *Holding the lid in the vise for ease of sanding*

Fig 4.27 *Taper the pegs, holding them flat on the bench with one hand as you work*

Fig 4.28 *A slicing cut is better than a straight push*

Fig 4.18

Fig 4.19

planed about 5° off
square so that the
lid is stopped just
beyond the vertical

1mm (½in) clearance

Fig 4.20

Fig 4.21

Fig 4.22

Fig 4.23

the lid tapers to about
8mm (⁵⁄₁₆in) at the front

Fig 4.24

Fig 4.25

Fig 4.26

Fig 4.27

Fig 4.28

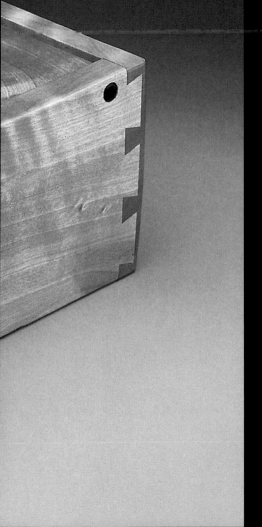

his came to be known as a tilt hinge box because the first one I made had the pivots about one-fifth of the way in from the back of the lid and there was no handle on it at all, you simply pushed the back and the lid tilted open. This meant that a lot of the space depth-wise was wasted, so I moved the pivots back and added a handle, but the name stuck.

THE WOOD

The wood I have chosen for this box is ripple silver birch which, in contrast with some of my other boxes, is a lovely, warm cream. Despite its fairly uniform color and figure it's still well worth inspecting the board carefully when you are marking out, and giving consideration to where even the smallest knot will be on the finished box. On part of the board I used, the ripple tended to run towards a point on the edge. I chose this piece for the lid and used the focus point of the ripple for the handle.

THE PROCESS

As described in Chapter 3, map out the front and sides of this box on the board. Cut each piece to width and cut the sides square and to length. Dovetail the corners.

The carcass

With the four sides assembled, make sure the carcass sits flat by standing it on a machine table or a piece of glass. Take the internal dimensions, add 11mm (³/₈in) to each – 5¹/₂mm (⁷/₃₂in) all round – and cut a piece of 4mm (⁵/₃₂in) plywood to this size for the base.

Cover this plywood in leather, either on one side only or on both, and then, using a pair of vernier calipers, measure the thickness of the base. Covering one side only means you don't need so much leather and you could argue that the underside has no need of a leather covering. My first boxes were only lined on the inside and I left the underside as sanded and finished plywood, which was, in effect, birch veneer. (I used birch-faced plywood.) I now stick leather to both sides – I think the base looks better, I don't have to sand and I don't have to worry about minor imperfections in the plywood.

Next, rout a groove to this thickness and 6mm (¼in) deep along the bottom of the front, back and sides of the box. Make sure the grooves are stopped on the front and back.

Fig 5.1 *PVA glue works well for gluing leather onto plywood*

Fig 5.2 *Vernier calipers in action*

Fig 5.3 *Grooves for the base*

Fig 5.1

Fig 5.2

Fig 5.3

On the inside of each side, measure in 9.5mm ($^3/_8$in) from the back, and 8.5mm ($^{11}/_{32}$in) down from the top. Mark a cross at this point to indicate the position of the pivot hole. I use two spacers for this so that they are exactly the same on either side. Drill the pivot holes using an 8.5mm ($^{11}/_{32}$in) lip-and-spur bit.

Sand all the inside surfaces to 400 grit and take the sharp corners off the groove. This helps the leather-covered plywood slip into it. If necessary, lightly hammer the edge of the leather to thin it slightly and help it slip into its groove.

As always, assemble and clamp the box dry before gluing up. Take it apart and then glue up. Check that it is square and, if necessary, angle the clamps slightly to bring it into square.

The lid

Next comes the fitting of the lid. My approach to this is very suck-it-and-see, but it works. Plane one edge of the lid carefully. It's best to start with an end-grain edge. Make sure that the edge is square to the face and straight before sanding it to around 120 grit, then check that it is still square and straight.

Next, plane the back edge and, by offering the lid up to the box, check it for fit. Sand to 120 grit and check again.

With the lid in place, mark a pencil line onto the lid directly from the box, both front and back, to align with the inner edge of the sides, then plane and sand down to this line.

With the back and sides now fitting, use a marking gauge to mark the position of the holes for the pivots onto the lid. Drill these holes to approximately 30mm ($1^1/_4$in) deep using an 8mm ($^5/_{16}$in) lip-and-spur bit.

Make the pivots in exactly the same way as for those in the desk box (see Chapter 4, p 43). Mine are bog oak and, although I tend to dislike black and white, I think that it works very well in this proportion.

Plane a radius on the top of the lid so that it just clears the back when it is opened.

With the lid pivoted in position, mark a line for the front edge of the lid, curving it outwards to form the handle. My handle was just over two-thirds along the lid; the lid was 295mm ($11^3/_4$in) long and the center of the handle was at 205mm (8in).

Using an Arbortech or chisels and surform, shape the underside of the lid so that the handle is reduced to about 8mm ($^5/_{16}$in) thick at the front. Sand the bottom of the lid to 120 grit, then double-check the line for the front edge. Now that you've shaped the underside of the lid, you should double-check the line which was on the lid top. Alright, I know it won't have moved, but it really is worth checking. Carefully cut just on the waste side of this line, with a band saw or bow saw.

Fig 5.4 Using a spacer to mark the position of the pivot hole

Fig 5.5 Marking the other dimension with a second spacer

Fig 5.6 Using a lip-and-spur bit to drill the pivot holes

Fig 5.7 Remove the sharp corners from the groove: the leather-covered base will slip in more easily

Fig 5.8 If it doesn't want to slip in, hammering the edge of the leather lightly will help

Fig 5.9 Always check your box with a squaring rod

Fig 5.10 The lid squared and correct on two sides

Fig 5.11 Marking the third side

Fig 5.12 Marking the pivot holes

Fig 5.13 Planing a radius on the back of the lid

Fig 5.14 The back edge of the lid must be radiused in order to allow clean movement

Fig 5.15 With more weight at the back than the front, the lid will feel and look better

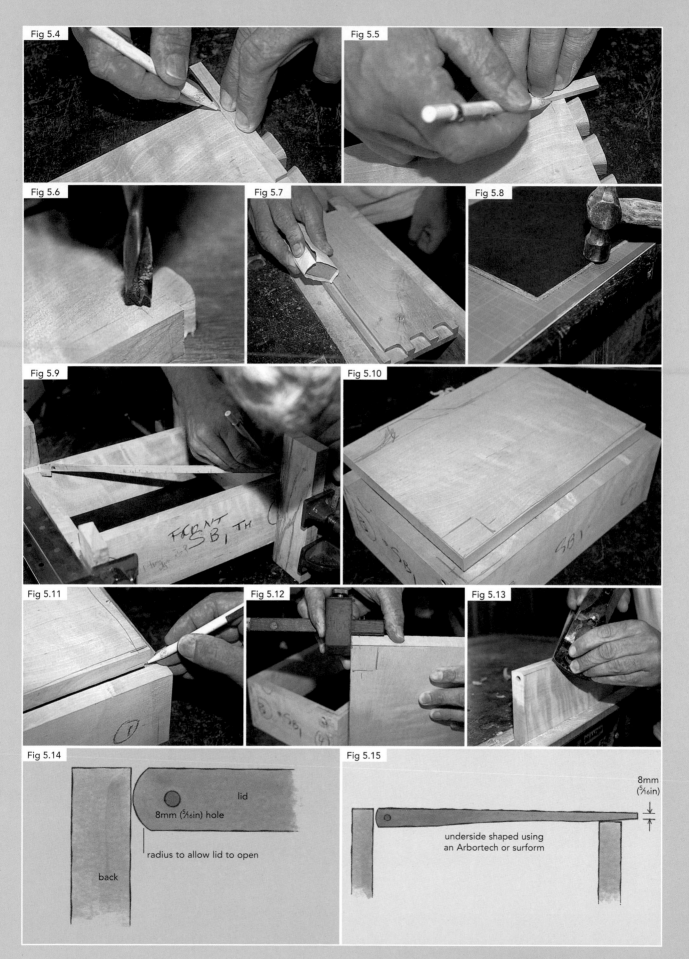

Fig 5.4

Fig 5.5

Fig 5.6

Fig 5.7

Fig 5.8

Fig 5.9

Fig 5.10

Fig 5.11

Fig 5.12

Fig 5.13

Fig 5.14

lid

8mm (⁵⁄₁₆in) hole

radius to allow lid to open

back

Fig 5.15

8mm (⁵⁄₁₆in)

underside shaped using an Arbortech or surform

Next, using a rasp, spokeshave or coarse sandpaper, work down to this line. Check it frequently with the pivots in place. When the front edge lines up perfectly with the front of the box, mark the handle onto the front of the box, then carefully remove the handle recess from the front of the box, using a backsaw and a chisel and sandpaper.

The handle

It is now a case of working a tiny bit at a time until the handle is a snug fit. If the recess is a little large, as long as the gap around the handle is even it will look fine. Place a strip of paper in the crack between the lid and box front and run it along; this will give a good indication of where the lid is tight. This is one of the most tedious parts of this box. It's not difficult, it just requires a lot of patience and concentration. Once this gap of paper thickness has been achieved the whole way along, the lid will fall with a very satisfying 'woomthf'. It is very tempting to take no more off and to leave it at that but unfortunately, the lid is subject to seasonal movement at best and, at worst, expansion or contraction as the wood settles down to the ambient moisture content. If the wood has been conditioned, then take a chance and leave the gap at paper thickness – about 0.2mm ($^1/_{100}$in). However, if there is any uncertainty concerning how wet (or dry) the wood is, increase the gap to around 0.5mm ($^1/_{64}$in).

Shaping

With the lid off, the box can now be shaped and finished. Finish the sides to a thickness of around 15mm ($^{19}/_{32}$in). I tend to curve the sides and ends very slightly to give a softer, more organic feel. Finish the whole box to 400 grit, rounding the outside edges but not the inside ones (those around the lid). Just take the sharpness off these with some 400 grit abrasive wrapped around a cork block.

The tray

The tray supports for this box are also of silver birch. Cut two pieces to 5mm ($^{13}/_{64}$in) thick. Measure the available height underneath the lid, subtract the height of the tray – in this case 35mm ($1^3/_8$in) – and glue in the two tray supports at either end of the box.

The tray itself is beech, which I think is sufficiently different from the birch to complement it; birch would be too soft for the fine dovetails on the tray, sycamore would be too similar in color and any darker wood would be too stark a contrast. The tray is 110mm ($4^3/_8$in), just under two-thirds the width of the box, which I think looks just about right.

Finishing

Finish the box in the usual way, keeping the lid separate, with three coats of Danish oil and then wax. Up to this point the lid has been pivoted

Fig 5.16 *Marking the handle on the front of the box*

Fig 5.17 *You will need to take several backsaw cuts before you begin chiseling*

Fig 5.18 *Chiseling the waste from the recess*

Fig 5.19 *Running a piece of paper around the gap will tell you where the lid is touching*

Fig 5.20 *Gluing the tray supports in position*

with two long pivots in order to make it easy to take on and off as you continue to work on the box. Once everything has been completely finished, push in the pivots, mark off their length, remove and cut them to size, then sand them on a disc sander to about 0.5mm (1/64in) beyond the mark, and very slightly convex. Finally, with a drop of glue in the hole, the pivots can be pushed home.

Fig 5.16

Fig 5.17

Fig 5.18

Fig 5.19

Fig 5.20

MITERED FINGER-HOLE BOX

For this box I chose to miter the corner joints rather than dovetail them because I wanted the black lines on the spalted beech to run right around it. Mitered joints tend to mean straight sides and sharp corners, so this piece has a different character from a lot of my others. The lid is shaped, but only on the underside, so the overall impression is of an ordered, geometrical box which I think contrasts well with the random lines of the spalting.

THE WOOD

I chose spalted beech for this box. Beech is 'the mother of the forest'. The fresh green of its foliage in spring, and the golden bronze in autumn make beech woods a beautiful sight. Beech is used for the wrest plank in pianos, which must bear the strain of 225 or more strings, each under a tension of more than 68kg (150lb).

I must admit to having slightly mixed feelings about using spalted woods. Strictly speaking, spalted wood is wood that is on its way to being rotten, and who wants a rotten box? I'm being pedantic of course. Spalted beech is very striking and if it's 'caught' in time – that is, before it has started to rot but after the fungus has started to spread – it can look gorgeous and still be perfectly sound. Random jet black lines flicker across the surface. The effect is brilliant.

There is a caveat, however. When working with spalted wood, the effect on your health may not be as brilliant as the appearance of the finished piece – the fungal spores can cause respiratory problems. Following the 'better safe than sorry' principle, it's a good idea to wear a mask and use some form of dust extraction when you're working with any spalted wood.

THE PROCESS

Map out your box, cut out all your pieces, and number the lengths of material before cutting the miters on each piece. If you've got a good and accurate miter box this will not be a problem. If you have a radial arm saw which will cut an accurate 45°, again, life is easy. I don't have a miter box and my radial arm saw is not that accurate, so I use a jig on my sanding disc. Of course, a shooting board for miters would also do the job.

The miters

Mark the miters on each piece and crosshatch the waste wood. It's surprisingly easy, once there are four pieces, to get mixed up and miter the wrong side.

Cut the miters with a backsaw or radial arm saw set to 45°, and finish them on the sanding disc. It is essential that the sides and ends are parallel as both edges will be used on the jig as a reference. To make sure that they are parallel, once they've been planed to the gauge line, clamp all four together in the vise, plane off a couple of shavings until they are spot-on equal, then reverse any two of the pieces. If they are even slightly out of parallel, this will show up. Keep planing and reversing until they are spot on.

The carcass

In order to measure for the base and to check that everything comes together, assemble the frame of the box dry. Lay the pieces flat on the bench, with their edges touching, and join them with two pieces of masking tape. The first three pieces can then be folded up to allow the final corner to be taped. If all your work is accurate, these joints will pull together without a gap.

Fig 6.1 *The waste is crosshatched and the miters roughly cut on the waste side of the line*

Fig 6.2 *The miters are finished on the sanding disc*

Fig 6.3 *Masking tape forms a 'hinge' on the corners, enabling the box to be folded up*

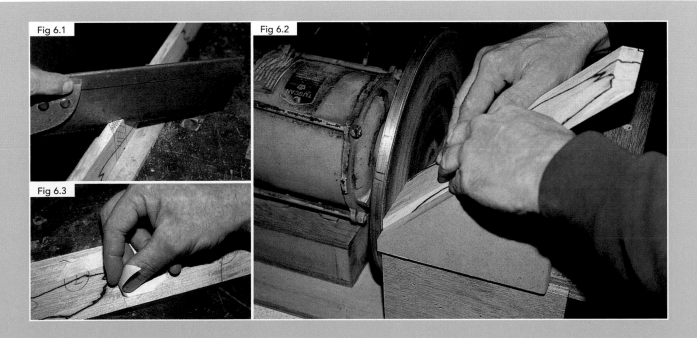

Fig 6.1

Fig 6.3

Fig 6.2

Measure the inside dimensions, add 11mm ($^7/_{16}$in), and cut a plywood base to this size. Cover the base with leather on one or both sides. (See Chapter 5, p 49.) Measure the thickness of the base, including the leather covering, disassemble the frame and rout a groove to this width, 6mm ($^1/_4$in) deep and 6mm ($^1/_4$in) in from the bottom edge of all four pieces. Next, re-position the fence to rout a 5mm ($^3/_{16}$in) groove for the lid stop along the front of the box, 6mm ($^1/_4$in) deep and 8mm ($^5/_{16}$in) down from the top.

For the hinge pivots, drill an 8mm ($^5/_{16}$in) hole, 10mm ($^{13}/_{32}$in) from the top and 15mm ($^{19}/_{32}$in) from the back of the box in each side.

The finger holes

The next job is to cut the finger holes; how depends entirely upon what equipment you have available. I tend to turn to the router for this sort of task. If you have a 22mm ($^7/_8$in) straight router cutter and a router mounted under a table, set a stop to position the finger hole and another stop to limit the distance of travel, and slide the side piece into the cutter. Failing a 22mm ($^7/_8$in) router cutter or a sliding fence, the holes can be drilled with a drill press. For this you will need to clamp a piece of waste material against the edge of the side and I would strongly advise that you clamp the whole thing down to the drill table.

Gluing up

Now sand all the inside surfaces to 400 grit. With this done, the box is ready to glue up. Lay the pieces out on the bench as before and tape them together with masking tape. Check that the leather-covered base fits snugly into its groove. If it is too tight a fit, hammering the edges lightly to thin the leather can make all the difference. For the gluing, use a slightly diluted PVA (about 1:10 water to glue). If the PVA is not diluted and you don't work very fast, it sometimes sets in a gelatinous lump which prevents the miters fitting tightly. To prevent the glue bleeding onto the inside of the box, brush it only onto the outer two-thirds of the joint. Blob a little glue into the grooves of the base, stand the base in one groove, then fold and tape the box up. The trick with masking tape is to stick it firmly to one piece and stretch it to just before breaking point before sticking it to the other piece. Add some more tape to each joint to increase the pressure and reinforce the tape. Using a squaring rod, check that the box is square. In theory it has to be, but in practice it might need a tiny squish across the diagonals to make it perfect. When all is well, put the box to one side to dry.

The lid

Now is the time to cut the lid stop to length and glue it into its groove. To make the lid, plane and sand one edge. Hold this finished edge

Fig 6.4 *Marking the position for the pivot holes*

Fig 6.5 *Routing the semicircular finger hole*

Fig 6.6 *Positioning the finger holes*

Fig 6.7 *Sanding the inside surfaces*

Fig 6.8 *It is a good idea not to spread glue onto the inner third of the joint*

Fig 6.9 *Stretching the masking tape and sticking it down on the final corner*

Fig 6.10 *Marking the lid stop to cut it to length*

Fig 6.11 *Marking the lid to width*

Fig 6.12 *Positioning the hole for the hinge pivot*

Fig 6.13 *Planing a radius on the back edge of the lid*

tight up against one side of the box and mark on a pencil line for the other edge directly from the box. Plane and sand carefully down to that line. With the lid slotted into the box, it's now possible to see exactly how much of, and where, the back edge of the lid should be planed. When you have finished planing, drill the holes for the hinge pivots. Use the same measurements for these as for the pivot holes in the box sides – 10mm ($^{13}/_{32}$in) down from the back and 15mm ($^{19}/_{32}$in) in from the end.

Next, plane a 14mm ($^9/_{16}$in) radius onto the back edge of the lid and check it for fit. The lid should just clear the back of the box as it is opened.

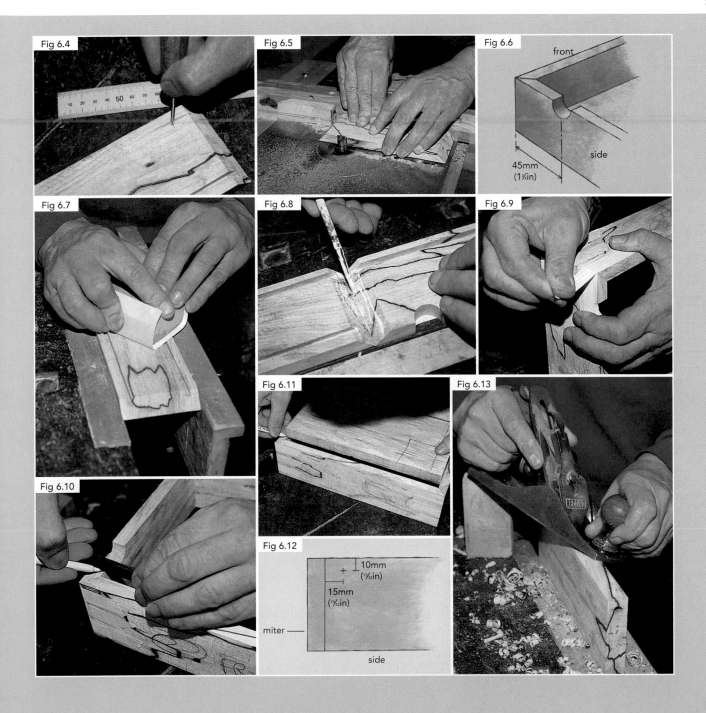

Fig 6.4

Fig 6.5

Fig 6.6
front
side
45mm
(1¾in)

Fig 6.7

Fig 6.8

Fig 6.9

Fig 6.10

Fig 6.11

Fig 6.12
10mm
(⅜in)
15mm
(⅝in)
miter
side

Fig 6.13

Once you are satisfied with the fit of the lid's sides and back, you can shape its underside. Use the Arbortech to remove most of the waste then move on to a surform with a curved blade, and finally, sand to a smooth, even curve finishing with a thickness of 8mm ($^5/_{16}$in) along the front edge.

The line of the front of the box can now be transferred onto the lid and the waste up to this line sawn and then planed off.

The splines

The miter splines are next. I've got a little jig that I use for holding rectangular boxes at 45° and recommend that you make one for this job (see Chapter 2). Using a long, 5mm ($^1/_4$in) straight cutter in the router, set the fence for the first line – the center of the spline, 15mm ($^1/_{32}$in) from the base. Set the cutter to about two-thirds the depth of cut required, cradle it in the jig, hold the box firmly against the fence and take the first cut, for the first slot, on all four corners. Increase the depth of cut to 16mm ($^5/_8$in) – this was the full length of my 5mm ($^1/_4$in) cutter – and take the final cut. Do not forget to set a stop to record the final depth.

Reset the fence to 32mm ($1^1/_4$in) from the base and cut the second slot in the same way. The third slot can be cut in the same way on the front but the back spline is shorter on the side than the back which, unfortunately, means making another cradle. I sat and wracked my brains trying to figure out a way of using the 45° jig, but it was a waste of effort. When I got down to it the second jig didn't take that long and it's definitely the best method.

I used little pieces of bog oak for my splines because the black went so well with the spalted beech. Plane a length of about 350mm (14in) to 22mm ($^7/_8$in) wide and 5mm ($^1/_4$in) thick. Check that both edges are absolutely square to the face, then cut out the triangular splines on alternate sides. These triangles should be a snug fit. They certainly shouldn't need hammering in and neither should they fall in. For each spline, brush a thin coating of glue into the groove and onto the spline and push it firmly home. Once the glue has hardened, the waste can be sawn off and then planed flush.

Finishing

Now sand the whole box, taking care to keep all the lines straight and crisp. When it comes to the corners and edges, just wave a piece of 400 grit abrasive in their general direction. Well, maybe one or two passes with a bit of worn 400 grit but no more than that. The finger holes can be sanded with abrasive wrapped around a dowel rod, preferably of a diameter just slightly less than the hole. I find half an old pool cue an excellent tool for this job as, being tapered, it fits most diameters. The box and lid can now be oiled. Spalted wood definitely requires more oil than most other woods: it tends to be

Fig 6.14 *Working on the underside of the lid with the Arbortech*

Fig 6.15 *Marking the lid exactly from the front of the box*

Fig 6.16 *Cutting the slots for the miter splines*

Fig 6.17 *My spline cradle for the short spline*

Fig 6.18 *Cutting the splines*

Fig 6.19 *Cutting bog oak triangles with a backsaw*

Fig 6.20 *Gluing in the splines*

Fig 6.21 *Cutting off excess spline slightly proud of the box*

Fig 6.22 *Sandpaper wound around a piece of pool cue*

Fig 6.23 *Fixing the dowels in place*

softer and more absorbant, and more or less drinks the first coat. Around four coats should do it. After oiling, apply a coat of beeswax in the usual way (see Chapter 3, p 28).

The dowels for the lid should be a good push fit. (See dowel cutter in Chapter 2, p 22.) Insert them into the holes and mark, with a sharp pencil, where they need to be cut.

Remove them from their holes, cut them off, then sand the ends to about 0.5mm (¹⁄₆₄in) beyond the pencil line. With this done, oil the end of the dowels.

Finally, using a stick of wood, put a drop or two of glue into the dowel holes, insert the dowels and push them home.

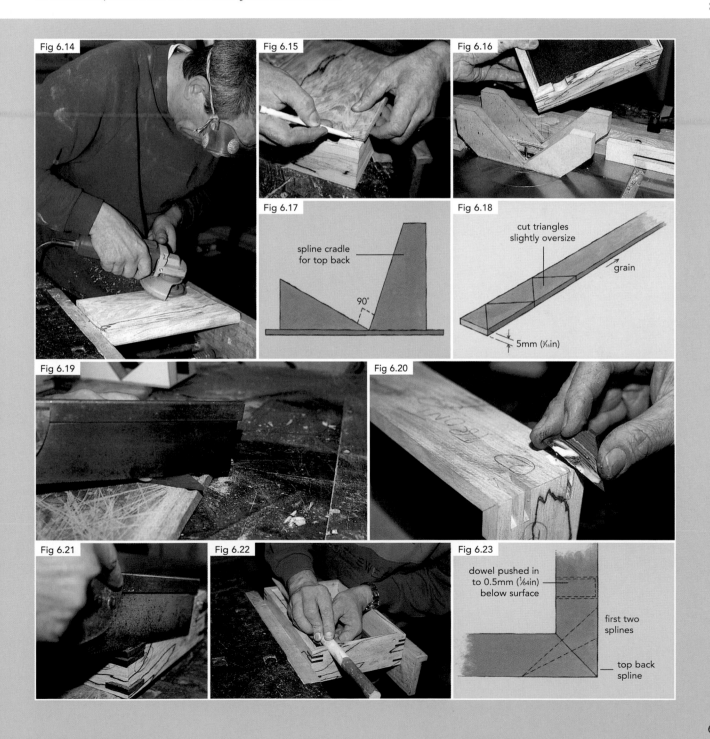

61

CASH BOX

I have to admit, the thought of making a cash box was not immediately appealing, so this one kept getting moved to the back of the line. Other boxes just seemed to push in front. I don't know if it was because I was unsure how to go about designing a box 'inspired by the Dales' or if it was the thought of my box, lovingly sanded with bucket loads of elbow grease, having money slung into it... Whatever it was, inspiration would not come. But I had been commissioned so I was duty-bound to produce.

The 'inspired by the Dales' bit did hold me up, but eventually that was exactly what happened. Thinking of hills and how often there is one behind another, I got to thinking that maybe something like that could be represented in wood. Maybe hills could be reflected in some sort of hinge. Could the burry bits represent the rocky outcrops? I almost got carried away.

I have deviated slightly from a vague central philosophy of mine in that I don't like unnecessary bits, bits that have no function. I like big hinges, I like dovetails and big handles and I'm quite happy to remove wood, but I don't like to add anything purely for decoration and strictly speaking, the middle and bottom 'hills' of this box aren't necessary. However, if there was only the top 'hinge hill', the box wouldn't be balanced and as for the middle pieces, they make excellent handles.

I have to say this box took me longer than I expected. I thought it would be a doddle, after all it was, in essence, a pivot hinge box and I'd made loads of those. But it managed to throw up some quite new problems.

It goes without saying that the insides of this box can be arranged to house virtually anything. Now, on with the box.

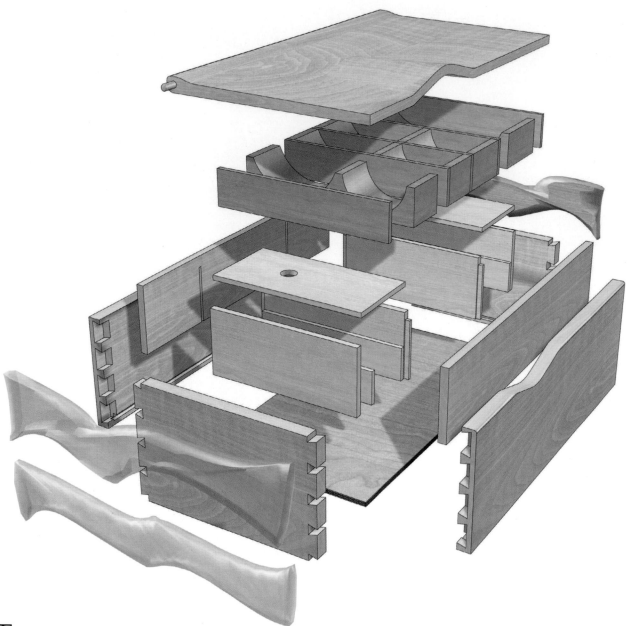

THE WOOD

For this box I chose wych elm. There are old country verses that seem not to care much for the elm family. According to these, not only do they deliberately drop branches on anyone silly enough to shelter under them, they don't even burn very well. However, a tiny piece dropped into the urn will foil witches in their attempts to prevent dairymaid's from churning milk to make butter.

In 1975 several English counties reported the death of 98% of all their smooth-leaved elms – the catastrophe of Dutch elm disease. Wych elm is also affected by this disease but is still holding its own in many places. 'Wych' means pliant or supple and the wood of the wych elm is stronger and worked more easily than that of other members of the elm family. Depending on the minerals present in the soil in which the tree grew, the wood often has a very pronounced green coloring.

THE PROCESS

Start by dovetailing a box of 450 × 260 × 150mm (18 × 10 × 6in).
I cut small dovetails at the top for additional strength: I had a vision
of the cash tray, loaded with coins, being bashed violently back and
forth, like a hammer on the inside of the box.

The carcass

Once the dovetails are cut, assemble the four sides and level
their bottoms with a try plane. Rout a 4mm ($^5/_{32}$in) groove on each
piece, 6mm ($^1/_4$in) in from the bottom edge and approximately 7mm
($^1/_4$in) deep. Cut a plywood base around 1mm ($^1/_{32}$in) undersize, glue
moiré to the base of the plywood, then glue up the box. Clamp it
with sash clamps, use a squaring rod to check that it is square, and
put it to one side for the glue to dry. Once it has dried, remove the
clamps, plane the ends flat, and plane and sand the top edge of the
box to 240 grit.

The hills

Now for the 'hills'. I cut my mock-ups in MDF but you could use card
to get an idea of shapes and how they would look. However, there is no
substitute for real wood with its figure and color. I tried to
translate an MDF shape straight onto a piece of elm and it just didn't
look right; you have to work with the swirls and shapes in the wood –
you can't cut across them.

Once you are happy with the shapes of the hills, identify them
clearly so that they don't get mixed up. I used At (top left) Am
(middle left) and Ab (bottom left) and Bt, Bm and Bb for the right-
hand side, but now I come to think of it, numbering them 1 to 6 would
have done just as well.

Raise the box about 25mm (1in) off the bench on a piece of wood,
and fix the hills in position with a couple of blobs of glue from a hot-
melt glue gun. Now you will start to get an idea of how they will look.

Fig 7.1 *Holding the hills against
the box will give you an idea of
what they're going to look like*

Fig 7.2 *Gluing the hills on with a
hot-melt glue gun*

Fig 7.1

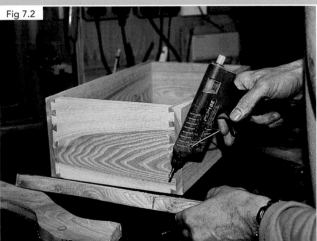
Fig 7.2

This is the time to mark the positions of the pegs to secure the hills. There should be at least two pegs per hill. I used five per side, which made six including the hinge pivot. The peg holes will prove very useful while you are making the box – as you will constantly be taking the hills on and off – and the pegs will add strength. Bear in mind that the middle ones will be used as handles for a potentially very heavy box.

For each peg, drill a 10mm ($^3/_8$in) hole through the top of the hill and into the side of the box. Do remember to set the depth stop – the thought of the drill bit emerging on the inside of the box fills me with horror. I used my drill press but an electric drill or a carpenter's brace would do just as well. For some reason – which I knew at the time but I'm blowed if I can think of now – I made my peg holes 5mm ($^1/_4$in), intending to increase them to 10mm ($^3/_8$in) at the very end of the project. With hindsight this was not a very good idea: to get a perfect entry hole when you are enlarging one, you need an extremely sharp bit.

Once your peg holes are drilled, mark the positions of the hinge pivots on the top hill. Using a spacer, mark these 11mm ($^7/_{16}$in) in from the top edge and 11mm ($^7/_{16}$in) out from the inside of the box. I used a piece of wood planed to 11mm ($^7/_{16}$in).

Trace around both sides of the middle hill onto the top and bottom hills with a soft-leaded pencil. Tap off the middle hill with a hammer and trace around the inside of the top and bottom hills onto the box. Tap off these two hills and crosshatch the area inside the lines to indicate which parts of the lid, top and middle hills will be overlapped. These areas must be left flat, but the rest of the hills can be shaped and sanded to your heart's content. Before setting to with the sanding, drill two 10.5mm ($^3/_8$in) holes for the hinge pivots.

These hills are not the easiest things in the world to pop into a vise. By using my bench dogs, and sometimes the vise, I was able to secure them, but you could find that the peg holes are useful for screwing them onto a bit of waste wood which, in turn, can be fixed to the vise. My 'dogs' are wooden stops, two of which are located in the jaw of the tail vise. The third, and sometimes a pair, can be set at various positions along the bench. They can be moved into different holes, raised and lowered as needed. Sand the hills to just beyond the pencil lines, up to 240 grit.

The cash tray

Now, on to the cash tray. I couldn't use anything like my normal tray design, which is not nearly strong enough. Cutting the tray from solid wood seemed the obvious way to go. I had some 50mm (2in) thick acacia in the workshop which went very well with the color of the wych elm, so I was in business.

Fig 7.3 *Drilling holes through the hills for the pegs*

Fig 7.4 *Marking on the positions of the hinge pivots*

Fig 7.5 *Marking where the hills overlap (outsides)*

Fig 7.6 *Marking where the hills overlap (insides)*

Fig 7.7 *Crosshatch the faces over the area where they touch*

Fig 7.8 *Crosshatch where the hills touch the box*

Fig 7.9 *Using bench dogs to secure the hills*

Fig 7.10 *Shaping the secured hills with the Arbortech*

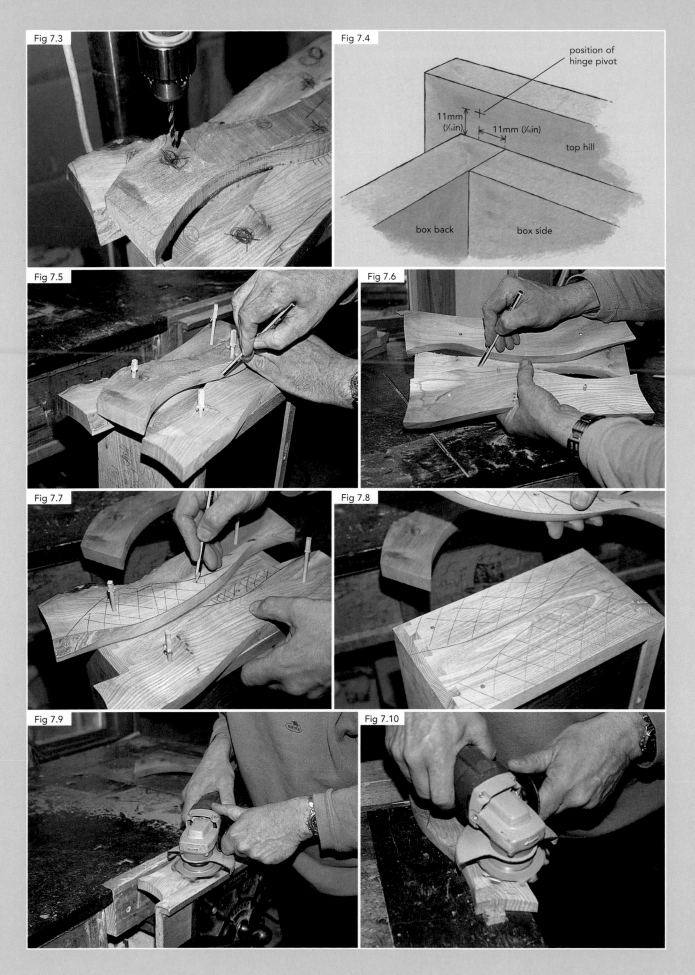

Fig 7.3

Fig 7.4

position of
hinge pivot

11mm
(⁷⁄₁₆in)

11mm (⁷⁄₁₆in)

top hill

box back

box side

Fig 7.5

Fig 7.6

Fig 7.7

Fig 7.8

Fig 7.9

Fig 7.10

Cut the acacia into four strips – two 55mm (2¼in) wide, one 68mm (2¾in), and one 82mm (3¼in) – each around 260mm (10in) long. This will give you 20mm (¾in) waste at either end. These must now be marked out for the coin scoops. There are six coin scoops and one larger bill scoop. The coin scoops are marked out using a compass to draw a radius on the edge of the strips. Rather than just picking a radius for these out of the blue, it's not a bad idea to give some thought as to how you are going to sand the radii. I found that a sanding drum designed to fit my radial arm saw was perfect for the smaller of the radii, and for the larger one I used the end drum of a belt linisher, which was 110mm in diameter. There are many other possibilities; a portable belt sander used carefully would do the trick, a foam drum sander would probably work and, indeed, a flapper wheel will do many different radii. It's important to leave at least 9mm (⅜in) of material on the bottoms when you saw them because, after they have been sanded on the insides and planed and sanded on the outside, their thickness can be markedly reduced.

Cut the radii using a 5mm (¼in) band saw blade; with a little patience a bow saw or a coping saw would do. Sand these, then plane the sides flat and square to the base.

For the dividers of the coin tray I used five strips of 7mm (⁹⁄₃₂in) burr elm. Cut these oversize in width by about 3mm (⅛in) and in length by about 10mm (⅜in) and sand the faces flat to 400 grit.

Now clamp the whole lot together, positioning sash clamps alternately on the top and bottom. Make sure the tray doesn't bow up or down, which may happen if there is unequal pressure from the sash clamps or if one or more of the faces are out of parallel. Once you are satisfied that the tray goes together snug and square, glue it up. You can quite happily spread the glue right up to the outside edges, but take care to keep it at least 5mm (¼in) away from the sanded insides: trying to clean up squish-out from the insides is not very easy.

To fit the tray, mark its sides to the width of the box, preferably with a knife line: this will prevent the wood from splintering under the saw cut. Saw the tray to width, plane it up to the knife line, then plane the bottom and top flat and sand the whole thing.

The runners and crosspieces

Now for the runners. First cut two pieces of 12mm (½in) acacia to fit the inside length of the box exactly. I used my normal suck-it-and-see approach for this. I cut them on the saw to about 0.5mm (¹⁄₆₄in) too long and then finished them on the sanding disc, a tiny bit at a time, until they slid down into a snug fit. I find it helps if I take the arris off the inside edge, though not right to the top where the radius would be seen. The width required is the depth of the box minus the thickness of the tray, plus 3mm (⅛in). The tray, which will slide along these runners, will then sit about 3mm (⅛in) below the top of the box. Sand the runners to 240 grit.

Fig 7.11 *Using a pair of dividers to mark out the radii*

Fig 7.12 *Cutting the coin scoops on the band saw*

Fig 7.13 *Sanding the coin scoops using a drum on the radial arm saw*

Fig 7.14 *Sanding the coin scoops using the end of the linishing belt*

Fig 7.15 *The coin scoops with the dividing pieces ready to be glued*

Fig 7.16 *Sanding the tray with a strip of abrasive paper wrapped around a block*

Fig 7.17 *The runners should slide into place with a snug fit*

Fig 7.11

Fig 7.12

Fig 7.13

Fig 7.14

Fig 7.15

Fig 7.16

Fig 7.17

runner

box back

box side

To determine the position of the two central crosspieces, place the tray first up against one end of the box and then the other, and mark a pencil line on each end of the runners, 3mm ($\frac{1}{8}$in) in from the end of the tray. These four marks are the centerlines for routing out the grooves into which the dividers will slot. Rout these grooves 5mm ($\frac{1}{4}$in) deep with a 3mm ($\frac{1}{8}$in) straight cutter.

Cut the two crosspieces 9mm ($\frac{3}{8}$in) over-length and cut the shoulders using a pair of slotting cutters on the router. Sand them to 400 grit and check that the runners and crosspieces go together. You should have a good tight fit. If you do, it's probably a good idea not to push the second runner right home for the moment: you may well not get it out again.

Once you're certain that the runners and crosspieces are going to slide home alright, glue the first runner onto the box side, dribble two lines of glue onto the base where the crosspieces will sit and a few drops into the grooves in the second runner, then dab a few blobs of glue onto the other box side and quickly push the second runner home. If it's a really good fit it might need a few gentle taps with a hammer, cushioned by a piece of waste wood. A clamp across the outside of the box may well be necessary to bring the shoulders up tight, and it's a good idea to use a couple of clamps to hold the base firmly onto the dividers as well.

At this point I decided that my box didn't look quite right. It seemed to want two more crosspieces at either end to look complete, so, against my better judgement – generally speaking I don't like anything that isn't functional – I added these two pieces. Cut these end pieces exactly to length (there is no need for a housing), sand them and push them home, possibly with the help of a few taps from a hammer.

To support the inside lids, four additional crosspieces are needed. These should be about 45mm (1$\frac{3}{4}$in) wide. Once you have got them to an exact fit, sand them, number them so that you know which piece fits where, and put them to one side.

Cut two pieces of 7mm ($\frac{1}{4}$in) thick acacia for the compartment lids and make these a reasonably snug fit in the outside compartments – 0.75mm ($\frac{1}{32}$in) play is about right. Too tight and there's no room for seasonal movement. Drill a 22mm ($\frac{7}{8}$in) finger hole about two-thirds of the way down the hills. I have a thing about thirds. I think anything, well almost anything, positioned at thirds looks better than at halves.

Sanding the inside lids

These lids can now be sanded. It's best to sand them after drilling because, even using a really good, sharp auger bit, there could be tear-out on the underside, which will need cleaning up. I used a flat bit and, even though I held them firmly on a smooth piece of waste wood, there was some tear-out to clean up on the underside.

Fig 7.18 *Cutting the grooves for the divider*

Fig 7.19 *Cross section through the side of the box*

Fig 7.20 *Cutting the tenon on the end of a crosspiece (divider)*

Fig 7.21 *One of the crosspieces being offered up to the runner*

Fig 7.22 *Positioning the runners and crosspieces*

Fig 7.23 *Checking the second runner for fit*

Fig 7.24 *Using a sanding block to make smooth the end crosspieces*

Fig 7.25 *Tapping home an end crosspiece using a piece of MDF*

Fig 7.26 *Positioning the finger hole*

Fig 7.27 *A compartment lid*

Fig 7.18

Fig 7.19

cash tray

front

runner

back

crosspiece

Fig 7.20

Fig 7.21

Fig 7.22

side crosspiece

back

runner

front

Fig 7.23

Fig 7.24

Fig 7.25

Fig 7.26

approx. one-third
of total length

centerline

Fig 7.27

The lid

Now on to the box lid. It was at this stage that I marked and drilled the holes for the hinge pivots. With the luxury of hindsight, I was crackers. If you drilled these earlier, when I suggested doing it, and not now, when I did it, your life will be a lot simpler.

Cut the lid so that it is a snug fit between the top hills. Hold the hills in position with sash clamps underneath them while you are fitting the lid. Plane the back edge of the lid so the back corners just touch the pivot holes. Using a marking gauge, mark the positions of the pivots on the ends of the lid – 11mm ($^{13}/_{32}$in) from the underside and back. Next, having made sure that the drill is in line with the back of the lid, drill two 10mm ($^3/_8$in) holes for the pivots. I used my drill press for this but I didn't entirely trust the machine vise. I checked it by putting a piece of straight rod in the drill chuck to make sure that it was parallel to the back of the lid.

Radius the bottom back edge of the lid and plane the top back edge at a slight angle so that it is held open at an angle of just over 90°.

The surface of the lid now needs to be shaped and sanded. To further reflect the Dales theme, I shaped a small hill with the Arbortech, about a third of the way along the lid, which coincided very effectively with a focal point of the figure on the front of the box.

Finishing

Cut three pieces of leather to size for the bottom of the box compartments. You'll get a better fit if it is about 0.5mm ($^1/_{64}$in) oversize rather than too small. Leather has a capacity for contracting as well as expanding – probably just as well or our skin would be cracking all the time. Glue the leather in with PVA or latex glue, then glue the lid supports in position.

The front and back of the box can now be sanded. I didn't shape hills on these – that might have been overdoing things a bit – but just gave them a gentle curve and rounded all the sharp corners. Shape the sides by hollowing out the area between the crosshatching. Now sand everything (if you haven't already done so) to 400 grit.

Mask off the crosshatched areas of the hills and box sides with masking tape and oil the whole thing with three coats of Danish oil, allowing a day to dry between each coat. (You don't want oil on a surface which will later be glued because it won't stick.) Apply a coat of wax using 0000 grade wire wool, then buff it off.

The hills can now be glued on. Position them using the pegs, glue and clamp them, then remove the pegs. When the glue has hardened, glue the pegs into their holes, cut them to 5mm ($^1/_4$in) overlong, and then facet them with a chisel.

Finally, fix the lid on by placing a drop of glue in the pivot holes, pushing the pegs home, and again, cutting and faceting them. Finish the ends of these pegs with a drop of Danish oil.

Fig 7.28 *End view showing one set of hills*

Fig 7.29 *Marking on the width of the box lid*

Fig 7.30 *Planing a radius onto the inside back edge of the lid*

Fig 7.31 *Masking off the areas to be glued*

Fig 7.32 *The oiled pieces, with masking tape removed*

Fig 7.33 *Gluing the hills into place*

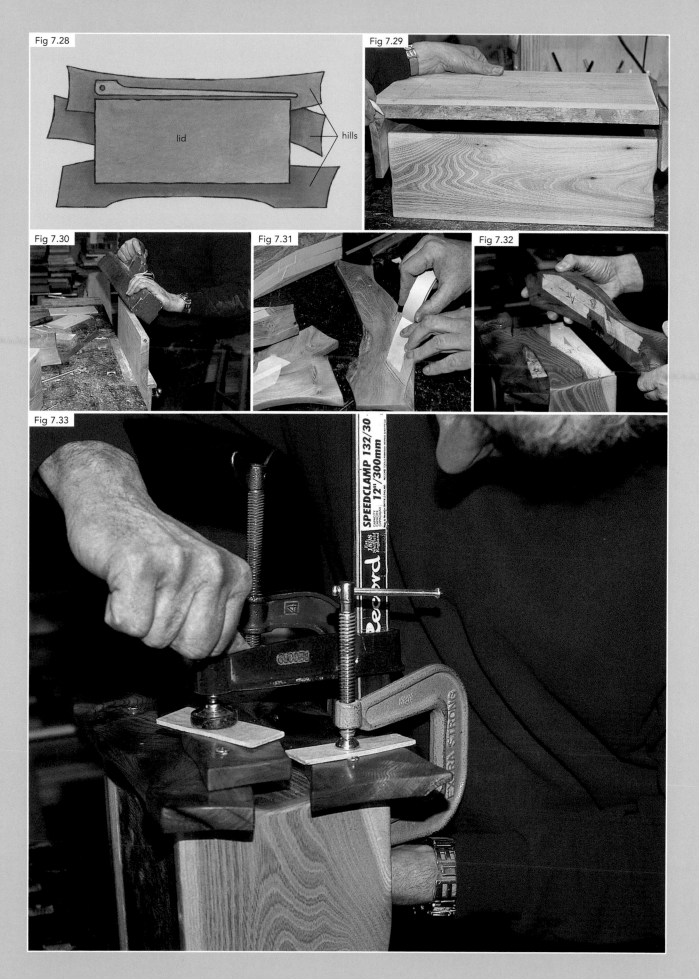

Fig 7.28

lid

hills

Fig 7.29

Fig 7.30

Fig 7.31

Fig 7.32

Fig 7.33

hen a customer asked me for a writing slope,
W the first thing that came into my mind was a
Victorian-style box that was pivoted in the center and
opened out to form a slope. Such boxes were carried by
ladies and gentlemen on their travels and contained
all they needed to pen letters back home from the far-
flung corners of the world – a forerunner to the laptop
computer. What my customer wanted though, was a fixed
slope with space for pens and paper to sit on his wife's
desk, providing a comfortable slope for writing. So the
thinking cap went on and this is the box that was born.

I've made several since this first one and people seem
to like them. Sometimes I think of them as an antidote
to computers; an alternative to that cold, hard, plastic
machine that buzzes and waits and stares back at you.

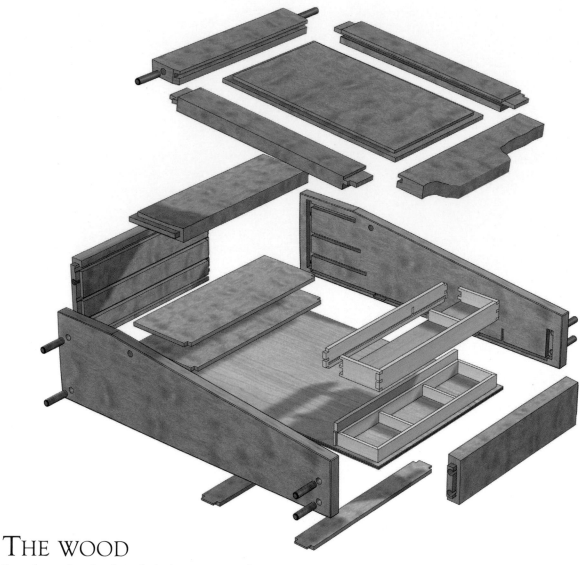

THE WOOD

I used yew for this box though it is certainly not the easiest wood in the world when it comes to planing. In fact, I think if I didn't have various sanding machines I would probably give it a wide berth.

Yew is a beautiful wood. When first cut it appears red, but turns brown on prolonged exposure. It is one of the heaviest of softwoods, noted for its resilience, and almost as hard as oak.

THE PROCESS

If possible, mark all the pieces on a single plank at least 1500mm (5ft) long and 18mm (³⁄₄in) thick: this allows the figure to run all the way around the box. If a board of this length is not readily available, try at least to map out the pieces so that the figure runs around the sides and front. The next most important consideration for this box is the lid panel. Choose the best section of plank for this; something with bold figure or swirling patterns in it. Bear in mind that the box will need to be visually balanced, for example, if there's a lot of close figure in the top left-hand corner, balance this by placing the handle in the bottom right.

At this stage of a box I usually spend time throwing down pencil lines, rubbing them out, re-positioning pieces, deciding what knots and defects I can use and working around those which I cannot.

The carcass

Once you have completed the mapping out, number and cut out each piece. It is often quite difficult to cut them precisely square and exactly to length at this stage, so it's a good idea to cut them all oversize. With this done, plane the bottom edge of each piece before planing them all to width, then cut the two sides, the front and back, the bottom supports, and the pencil holder precisely to length. At this stage, the slope is not cut and the lid frame and panel are both left oversize. Cut the stopped housings as described for the desk box (see Chapter 4, p 40).

Using a 5mm ($^{13}/_{64}$in) straight cutter, rout a groove for the base 6mm ($^{1}/_{4}$in) deep and 9mm ($^{3}/_{8}$in) from the bottom edge on all four sides. Check this groove using a piece of plywood with an offcut of leather glued to it. Generally, the leather I buy for boxes is about 1mm ($^{1}/_{32}$in) thick, and I stick this onto 4mm ($^{5}/_{32}$in) plywood. I say 4mm ($^{5}/_{32}$in) but plywood sold as 4mm is usually around 3.6mm ($^{9}/_{64}$in). It should be a snug fit, just able to slide. If necessary, adjust the fence and take another pass, then, using the same cutter, adjust the router fence and rout out the grooves for the two shelves. Check the fit once more – it's a great deal easier to widen a groove fractionally than to sand or plane a shelf. Use the same cutter to rout the groove for the pen holder. (See Fig 8.3 for the layout of grooves in the side pieces.)

Fig 8.1 *Mapping out the pieces*

Fig 8.2 *Make sure the figure in the lid panel and the handle balance visually*

Fig 8.3 *The layout of grooves on the side pieces*

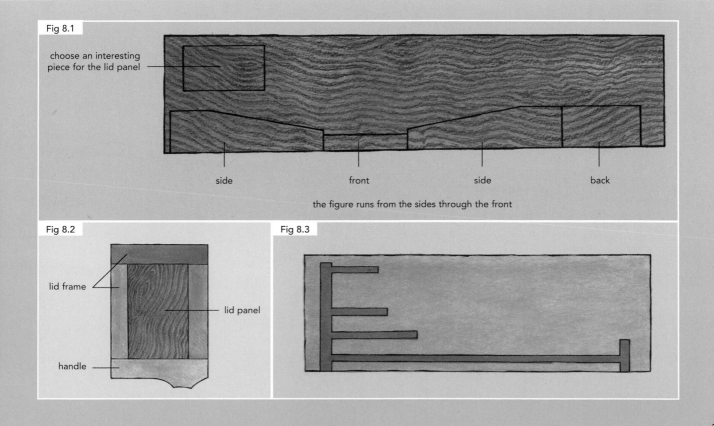

Fig 8.1

choose an interesting piece for the lid panel

side   front   side   back

the figure runs from the sides through the front

Fig 8.2

lid frame

lid panel

handle

Fig 8.3

Next, chisel the mortises for the base supports to the same depth as the groove. Take the length of the base supports from the front of the box as the two should be equal. Cut the tenons on the base supports in the traditional way, with a backsaw and chisel, or, as I often do, on the radial arm saw with a stop clamped to the fence.

The shelves

The next job is to cut the shelves. I made mine from sycamore which had been planed and sanded so that, after a final rub with 400 grit abrasive, they were a snug fit in the 5mm ($^{13}/_{64}$in) groove. Note that the bottom shelf is slightly wider than the top. It's a good idea to take the measurement for the shelves from the back or front piece as for the base supports. Cut the shoulder about 3mm ($^{1}/_{8}$in) longer than the groove: this allows for a little movement in the years to come. Make sure the shoulders come up against the sides of the box before the shelves hit the bottom of the grooves.

The pen tray

Now it's back to the router to cut the pen tray. Cut the rabbets – on three sides of the tray only – using a straight cutter. Do not take too much off in one pass. To remove any tear-out which might have occurred, make sure the final cut is with the grain. Remove the first 15mm ($^{5}/_{8}$in) of the tongue using first a backsaw and then a chisel, bevel-side up.

The front edge of the pen tray needs shaping to a radius and a straight edge to act as a stop. The easiest way of doing this is to use a box cutter with a 25mm (1in) diameter core on the router. Failing that, coarse abrasive wrapped around a block would take a little longer but would certainly do the trick.

The pen tray can now be shaped to a slight hollow using a surform followed by abrasive, or the Arbortech.

The front divider

Now, to the router table once more to cut the housing for the front divider. Again, I used sycamore planed and sanded to 5mm ($^{13}/_{64}$in). Make the housing trench 3mm ($^{1}/_{8}$in) rather than the full 5mm ($^{13}/_{64}$in): cutting shoulders on the divider will result in a much cleaner line.

The next piece to cut is the front divider. This involves working very precisely on a fairly small piece of material. The length between the shoulders must be exactly the same as all the other crosspieces – 230mm (9in). Accurate marking with a knife followed by careful paring with a chisel is probably the best way to cut these shoulders. An alternative is to cut them on the router table using either a straight cutter from both sides or an arbor and slotting cutters, with exactly the right spacer between them; in this way the job can be done in one pass (see trays in Chapter 3, p 28).

Fig 8.4 *The mortise on the side piece to take the base support*

Fig 8.5 *Cutting the mortise for the base support*

Fig 8.6 *The two shelves are cut to length and slotted into grooves in the sides and end pieces*

Fig 8.7 *The tenons on the base support can be cut on the radial arm saw*

Fig 8.8 *Cutting the rabbets on the edge of the pen tray*

Fig 8.9 *Plan view of the shelf and its groove in the side piece*

Fig 8.10 *Sanding the radius on the edge of the pen tray*

Fig 8.11 *The pen tray*

Fig 8.12 *Section through pen tray*

Fig 8.13 *All of the pieces in position; at this point the base has only an offcut of leather on it*

Fig 8.4

chisel mortises to same depth as groove

Fig 8.5

Fig 8.6

Fig 8.7

radial arm saw blade

bottom support

stop

Fig 8.8

Fig 8.9

depth of rabbet slightly less than depth of groove

Fig 8.10

Fig 8.11

Fig 8.12

planed to act as a stop for the lid

shaped to a slight hollow for pens

Fig 8.13

The lid

Plane the back and both sides of the lid frame to width and then, with all four pieces of the lid frame and the lid panel laid out on the bench, make a final decision about the shape of the handle. Mark each piece to identify how they all fit together by drawing a triangle on the lid and a part-triangle on each section of the frame as shown in Fig 8.15.

Square a knife line for the shoulder line around each end of the lid side pieces, add 20mm ($^7/_8$in) for the tenons and cut them to length. To prevent the front and back pieces of the lid from getting damaged if they're dropped or bashed, these are best left overlong at this stage.

Sand the inside edge of the frame pieces to 240 grit, making sure that they remain square. If you have a long-reach cutter, use it to rout a 5mm ($^{13}/_{64}$in) groove to a depth of 7mm ($^1/_4$in) on the inside edge of all four of the frame pieces. A standard 5mm ($^{13}/_{64}$in) straight cutter will do the job perfectly well but using a long-reach cutter will save having to deepen the mortises by hand later on.

The tenons can now be cut. This can be done with a backsaw, cutting by hand, or with the radial arm saw. If you do cut them by hand, use a mortise gauge to extend the grooves to the shoulder lines. If you use a radial arm saw, set the depth of cut carefully to the groove and clamp a stop to the fence for the first cut on the shoulder line. Take several passes across each tenon from one side, turn them over, re-set the depth of cut, and repeat. The tenons can then be finished using a broad chisel.

If you used a long-reach cutter for the groove you can deepen it to 20mm ($^7/_8$in) for the mortises in two or three stages. Otherwise, a fairly quick way of removing the bulk of the material is to hold the frame piece in the machine vise, set the depth stop of the drill press and, with a 5mm ($^{13}/_{64}$in) bit, drill several holes. You will then have to clean out the bottom with a chisel.

Mark out the haunches carefully – if you plane a piece of wood to the correct width it will save you measuring every time – and use a backsaw, or better still a fine dovetail saw, to remove the waste.

Assemble the frame and check that all the joints are absolutely tight and square before measuring the inside dimensions. Add 10mm ($^3/_8$in) to these all around and cut the panel for the lid to size and precisely square. Using a straight cutter with a diameter greater than 6.5mm ($^1/_4$in), cut a 6.5mm ($^1/_4$in) rabbet to a depth of 4mm ($^5/_{32}$in) all around the top of the panel. It is important that the end grain is cut first. The tear-out this causes will be removed later when you cut with the grain. Turn the panel over and, without altering the fence, cut the rabbet on the other side to leave a tongue of 5mm ($^{13}/_{64}$in). You might need to do this in two passes, depending on the thickness of the material. It is a good idea to cut the top rabbet on a scrap piece of the same material so that when it comes to cutting the bottom rabbet, the tongue can be checked in its groove and the depth set to achieve a

Fig 8.14 *Checking the appearance of the lid frame*

Fig 8.15 *Marking the lid frame*

Fig 8.16 *Use a knife line to mark the shoulders*

Fig 8.17 *The side of the lid frame showing tenon and haunch*

Fig 8.18 *Rabetting the lid panel*

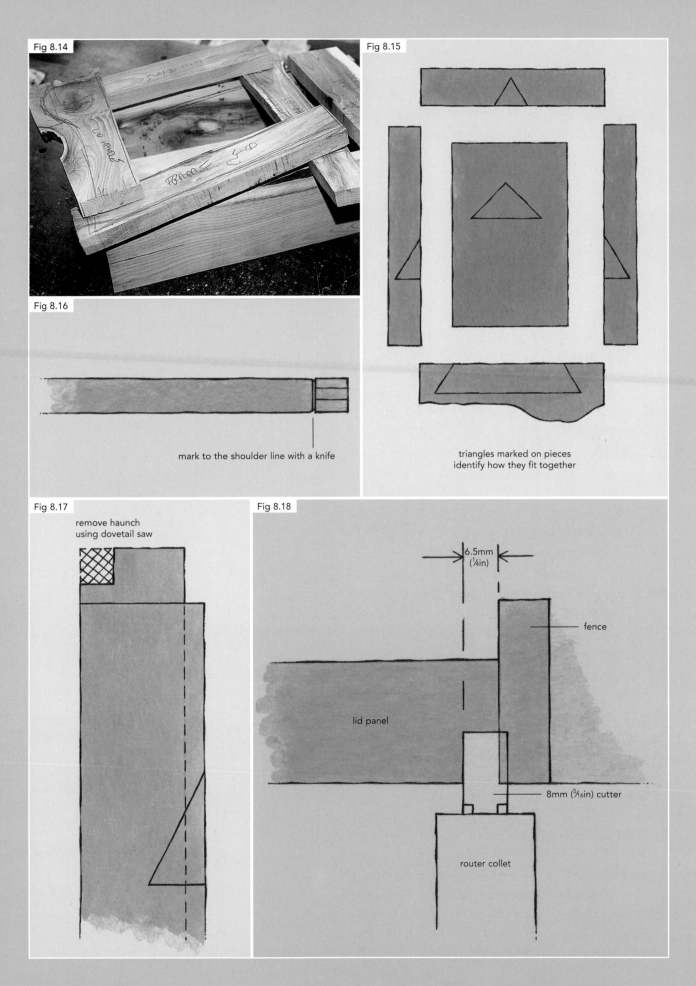

Fig 8.14

Fig 8.15

Fig 8.16

mark to the shoulder line with a knife

triangles marked on pieces
identify how they fit together

Fig 8.17

remove haunch
using dovetail saw

Fig 8.18

6.5mm
(¼in)

fence

lid panel

8mm (⁵⁄₁₆in) cutter

router collet

good snug fit. It shouldn't be so tight that it has to be hammered in nor so loose that it shakes from side to side.

Now check the panel in its frame, then shape and sand its underside. You can either plane this down to 14mm (⁹/₁₆in) and then sand it or slightly hollow the surface with an Arbortech and then sand to 400 grit.

With this done, the lid frame can be glued up. Spread the glue very thinly on the inside edge of the tenon – it is very difficult to remove any glue that squeezes into the groove between the panel and frame – and a little more generously on the outside edge. Do not glue the whole of the panel into the frame; a little glue in the center of the front and back is sufficient and will allow the panel to contract and expand with seasonal variations in humidity.

To keep the panel centered in the frame while you apply the clamps, it's a good idea to use a spacer. A plastic draft excluder does the job for me but any plastic object around 1.5mm (¹/₁₆in) thick, or pieces fixed together to make up that thickness – a margarine container or liquid-soap bottle – would do just as well. When applying the clamps, make sure they don't pull the frame out of shape in either the horizontal or the vertical plane. If the frame is not parallel with the panel, angle the clamps slightly to pull it into square. Leave the frame on one side to let the glue go off.

Back to the box

The holes for the lid can now be drilled. Fit the pen holder into its groove on the side piece, position it 1.5mm (¹/₁₆in) in from the back piece and, using the pen holder as a reference point, mark the position for the center point of the 8.5mm (¹¹/₃₂in) hole. The pen holder must be exactly parallel so that the hole for the pivot on the other side is marked in the equivalent place. The best way to get these holes drilled in the same place on each side is to mark out one side and drill it, and then hold the two sides together to mark out the other side, with the drill bit – preferably a lip-and-spur bit. If you are using a drill press you can clamp the sides to the table and drill the two pieces together.

The box can now be assembled dry. It will look a little strange because the slope on the sides has still to be cut. However, progress is being made.

The lid pivots

Plane the lid frame so that it tapers down to 14mm (⁹/₁₆in) at the front. The back needs the full thickness of the material for strength around the pivot but the front would look very heavy if it was left 18mm (³/₄in) thick. The extra length on the front and back of the lid frame can now be sawn off and the sides planed down to exactly 230mm (9in) so that it is a tight fit in the box. Push the lid in between the two sides and check that the top of the lid lines up with

Fig 8.19 *Do not apply any glue beyond this point on the lid frame*

Fig 8.20 *Gluing up the lid frame*

Fig 8.21 *Use sash clamps on both sides so that the pressure is equal and the joint is not pulled out of flat*

Fig 8.22 *Positioning the sash clamps to keep the panel centered*

Fig 8.23 *The position of the pivot hole relative to the edge of the pen holder, which is used as a reference*

Fig 8.24 *The lid is tapered at the front to a width of about 14mm (⁹/₁₆in)*

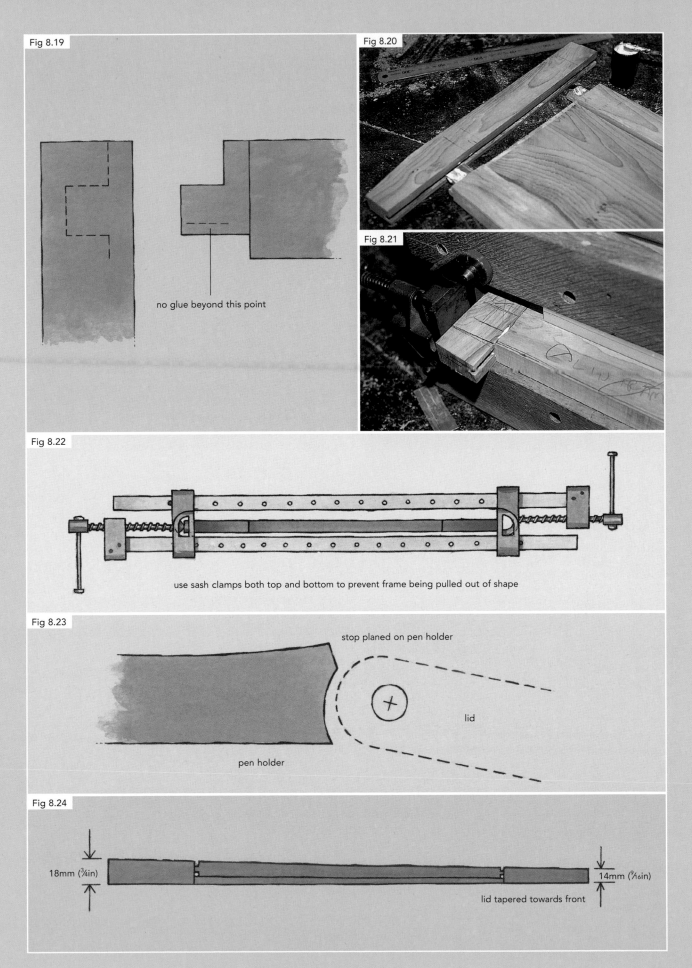

Fig 8.19

no glue beyond this point

Fig 8.20

Fig 8.21

Fig 8.22

use sash clamps both top and bottom to prevent frame being pulled out of shape

Fig 8.23

stop planed on pen holder

lid

pen holder

Fig 8.24

18mm (¾in)

14mm (⁹⁄₁₆in)

lid tapered towards front

the two pivot holes. If everything has been made good and square, it should need only minimal adjusting with a plane to achieve this.

The holes for the pivots can now be marked out on the lid. These 8mm ($^5/_{16}$in) holes can be drilled using a drill press, with the lid held in the machine vise, or using a wheel brace or power drill, with a square stood up on the bench for a vertical reference.

Next, make the lid pivots following the method described for the desk box (see Chapter 4, p 43).

Plane a slight radius on the back edge of the lid. The exact size for this radius is best found through trial and error. Finally, pivot the lid in position. You can now check the stop on the pen holder and, if necessary, plane it slightly so that the lid is held at about 80°.

Sanding and final shaping

Now sand the lid and all of the box pieces, except the outside of the sides, to 400 grit. It's also a good idea to take off the sharp edges of all the grooves as the leather may catch on them – anything that helps at the gluing up stage is definitely worth doing.

Assemble the front, back and sides of the box and pivot the lid. Now, finally, the slope of the lid can be marked onto the sides and cut. This slope could have been cut earlier – it could even have been cut right at the very start – but a wedge-shaped piece of wood is so much more difficult to hold in the vise. Put the offcut to one side: it will be useful later.

The leather can now be stuck onto the base. Cut it oversize, glue it using a slightly diluted PVA (about 1:10 water to glue), then trim it with a knife.

Assembly

The gluing-up stage has finally been reached. With the base supported on the bench on a piece of solid, clean plywood, hammer the edge of the leather. This thins out the edges which will help enormously when it comes to assembly.

A dry run is essential. Assemble the whole box, without the lid, and clamp it up. If at all possible use six sash clamps, two at each end and one for each bottom support. Using a pair of wedges under the bottom sash clamps, force the bottom supports upwards towards the base, to make them slightly concave.

Allow plenty of time, take the phone off the hook, hang up the 'do not disturb' sign and glue the box up. Repeat the hammering of the leather: it will have sprung back to some extent. Work fairly quickly, taking care to spread the absolute minimum of glue where it might squeeze out onto a sanded surface. The shelves and the pen tray need only a little glue in the back groove. Dab a little glue in the center of both bottom supports. The base itself needs only a few beads of glue dabbed at intervals along the length of the groove.

Fig 8.25 *The pen holder acts as a stop for the lid*

Fig 8.26 *Abrasive wrapped around a block is used to remove the sharp edges from the grooves*

Fig 8.27 *Rounding off sharp edges reduces the chances of the leather catching in the grooves*

Fig 8.28 *Hammering the edge of the leather will thin it slightly; it tends to spring back later and fill the groove*

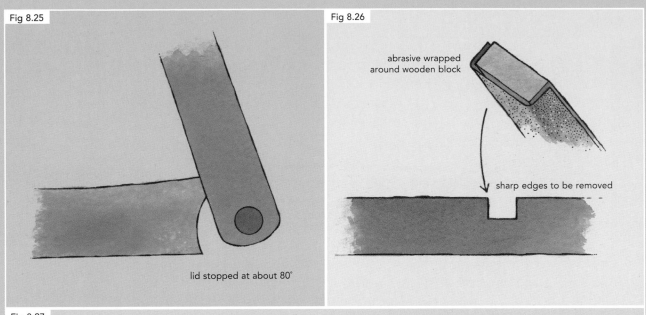

Fig 8.25

lid stopped at about 80°

Fig 8.26

abrasive wrapped around wooden block

sharp edges to be removed

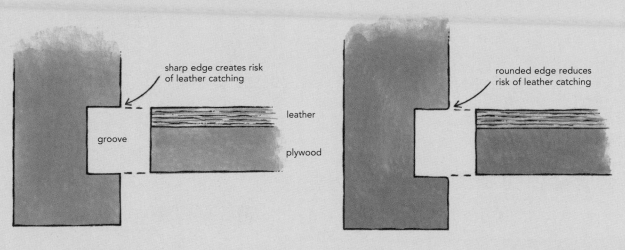

Fig 8.27

sharp edge creates risk of leather catching

groove

leather

plywood

rounded edge reduces risk of leather catching

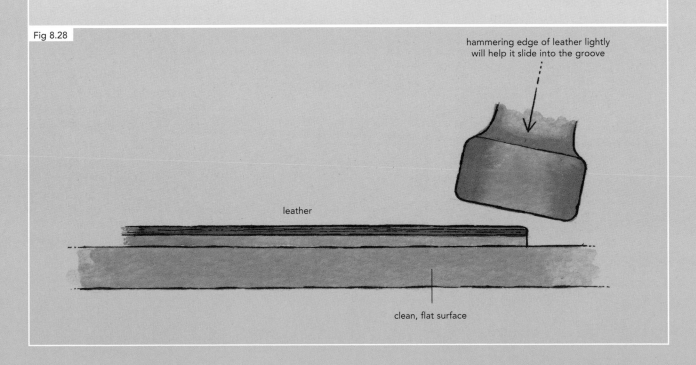

Fig 8.28

hammering edge of leather lightly will help it slide into the groove

leather

clean, flat surface

If everything is pulling up tight and there seem to be no problems, the sash clamps can go on. If there does seem to be a problem and something is not pulling up, it's important to investigate why, even though it's very tempting to get the clamps on and hope that sheer force will sort out the problem. It could well be that the leather has rucked up and is preventing the base from sliding into its groove or that one of the other pieces is not aligned properly.

Once the clamps are on, check that the box is square, using a squaring rod. If necessary, skew the clamps slightly to bring it into square. Don't forget to check that the pen holder is square and centered.

There's definitely light at the end of the tunnel now. Check that the lid still fits between the sides. If it was a good tight fit before the box was glued up, it will almost certainly need reducing in width now. Taper the width very slightly towards the front so that even with slight movement in years to come, the lid will never bind on the sides.

The reinforcing pegs

Mark a line square up from the base (ie, at 90° to it) in line with the center of the housing joint. Mark the positions of the pegs on this line and, using an 8mm (⁵/₁₆in) bit, drill holes to a depth of about 20mm (⁷/₈in).

Using the wedge-shaped offcut to hold the box in the vise, shape and sand the sides. Hammer home the tapered pegs and chisel off the facets. (See Chapter 4, p 44.)

The tray

Cut four pieces of sycamore for the pen-tray supports and miter these into the front of the box. Cut dividers to separate this bottom compartment into three in the same way as you cut the front divider (see p 78). It will look much neater if you make these pieces about 3mm (¹/₈in) lower than the tray supports.

Following the instructions given for making trays in Chapter 3 (see p 28), make the tray.

Finishing

With this done, give the box three coats of Danish oil before waxing. The lid can now be fitted for the last time. Drop a touch of glue into the pivot hole, insert the pivots, saw off the excess and facet the ends.

As a finishing touch, using a punch and a drill bit the same size, fit leather discs to the underside of each corner. Alternatively, it is possible to buy discs of felt.

Fig 8.29 *Mark the positions for the reinforcing pegs*

Fig 8.30 *The sides are shaped so that they are slightly convex*

Fig 8.31 *A painting box that I made along the same lines as the writing slope for a customer who painted miniatures*

Fig 8.32 *Detail of painting box showing storage for brushes*

Fig 8.33 *Detail of painting box showing storage for work in progress beneath the lid*

Fig 8.29

Fig 8.30

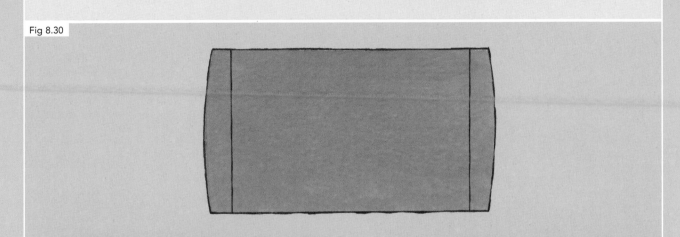

Fig 8.31

Fig 8.33

Fig 8.32

STRAP HINGE

*'These are the sort of boxes which hobbits would own', somebody once told
me at an exhibition. Another admirer thought that they were more
Walt Disney. Whatever they remind you of, the big strap hinges are larger
than life and these boxes certainly can't be ignored.*

*I think these hinges are especially suitable for burry woods, or woods
with a lot of character. The boxes themselves are fairly straightforward – it's
the hinges and the wood that make them. The hinges are also the part
over which most care needs to be taken. They may look large and none
too precise but if they are not made and positioned very
accurately they can present big problems.*

Work box
p 91

Stationery box
p 105

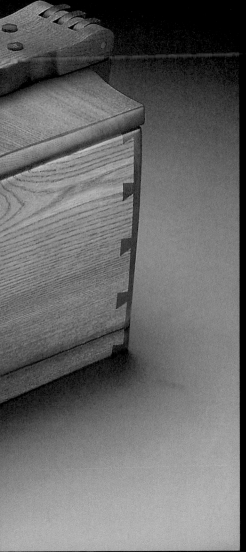

one. Some were fabric and hung beneath the table, some were on a stand and others were simple boxes. However, recently, possibly because leisure time is increasing, I've noticed a resurgence in the demand for work boxes. In its simplest form, a work box is somewhere to keep a selection of buttons and threads, a box of pins, and some needles. Now though, it seems that people who want work boxes are often serious embroiderers or needleworkers who want to keep embroidery threads, tapes, scissors, pins and needles in the box along with their work in progress – this obviously requires extra space.

I was commissioned to make just such a box with overall dimensions of $550 \times 290 \times 200$mm ($220 \times 11^{1}/_{2} \times 8$in).

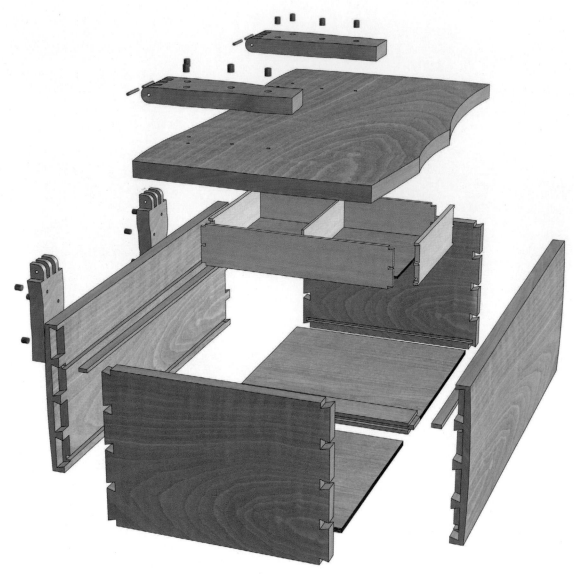

THE WOOD

From my stock of planed burr elm planks I selected one which was wide enough for the lid and long enough for all four sides plus the lid, ie 2350mm (96in). The board was 21mm (⁷⁄₈in) thick. My client wanted burr elm but 'not too burry'. It was almost painful to waste some of the lovely gnarled edges.

THE PROCESS

I mapped out my box on the wood in order to leave room to take the hinges from above the sides and ends (the front and back). Mark the wood out in this way and make sure the front and back are labeled and that the joint is at the back.

It's always a good idea at this stage to check the back of the board very carefully. I have, more than once, carefully marked out a box only to find, sometimes even after cutting, that the back was badly marked in a critical place. This is particularly pertinent when using burr woods. Sand the back of the board to 220 grit.

The carcass

Cut the plank into the seven main pieces. Leave the lid and hinge pieces to one side for the moment.

If the edge of the board is perfectly straight and the ripsaw and crosscut saw used were perfectly set up, you will need do little more to the box parts than check that they are identical in size. However, in my workshop things are seldom that perfect. Plane the bottom edge straight and square then, using a square and working from the bottom edge only, check the ends and plane or shoot as necessary. Because the top edge is not used as a reference point, as long as the width is roughly correct, it can be ignored for the time being.

Now is the time to cut the lapped dovetails (see Chapter 3, p 30). Assemble the four sides and, by placing them on a flat surface – a machine table or a piece of glass – make sure that the bottom is flat. If it is not, carefully plane it down.

The base

This box is large enough to warrant a central bar to provide additional support for the base. For this I cut a piece of elm 300 × 30 × 15mm (12 × 1¼ × ⅝in). A 5mm (¹³⁄₆₄in) groove provides for a 4mm (⁵⁄₃₂in) plywood base plus 1mm (¹⁄₃₂in) of leather. Using the

Fig 9.1 *The box mapped out*

Fig 9.2 *The different pieces are identified by penciled numbers*

Fig 9.3 *The groove for the base is stopped; if this wasn't done, it would show as a square hole when the box was assembled*

Fig 9.4 *Cutting the groove for the base piece*

Fig 9.5 *The base support bar with grooves cut for the base pieces*

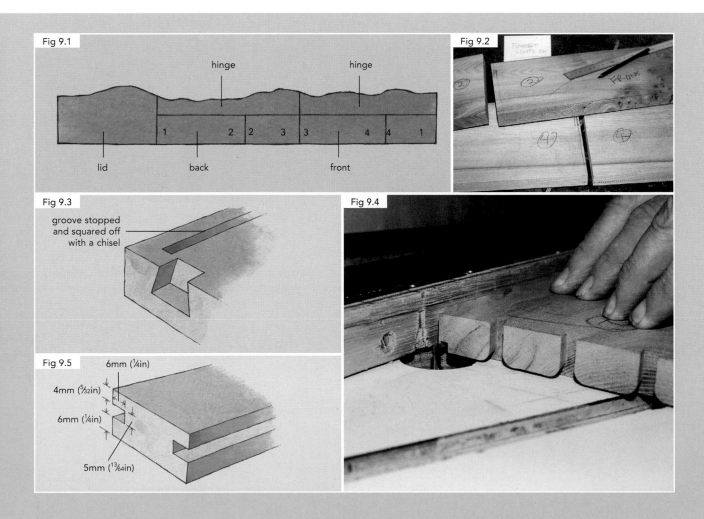

Fig 9.1

hinge · hinge

1 | 2 2 | 3 3 | 4 4 | 1

lid · back · front

Fig 9.2

Fig 9.3

groove stopped and squared off with a chisel

Fig 9.4

Fig 9.5

6mm (¼in)

4mm (⁵⁄₃₂in)

6mm (¼in)

5mm (¹³⁄₆₄in)

router with a 5mm ($^{13}/_{64}$in) cutter, route a groove 6mm ($^1/_4$in) in from the edge of the sides, front and back, to a depth of 6mm ($^1/_4$in), taking care that it does not show on the ends of the front and back; this will depend on the position of the dovetails. If the groove emerges in a tail then it can be run through. If it doesn't then it must be stopped on the front and back. The chances are that the first dovetail will not be low enough for the groove to emerge in a tail so it will probably have to be stopped.

In the same way, cut grooves on either side of the support bar. I cut the tenons on the end of the support using a stop on the fence of the radial arm saw, but they could equally well be cut, after careful marking out, with a backsaw and chisel.

You now need to cut two pieces of 4mm ($^5/_{32}$in) plywood for the base. The base is divided into two for this box as there would otherwise be a slight chance of sagging in the future. It's a good idea to sand one side (the bottoms) to 400 grit before cutting these to size: it's easier to sand one piece and not to have to worry about the edges. The two base pieces should be 249 × 258mm ($9^3/_4$ × $10^3/_{16}$in). Check the actual measurements with the assembled box. Always make the base smaller by 1mm ($^1/_{32}$in) all around. This is not so much to allow for movement, though for a solid wood base movement would have to be taken into account, but to allow for slight errors. It's a horrible feeling discovering that the base is slightly large when you have glue already on the joints and clamps waiting on the bench.

Assemble the box and double-check for movement in the base. It's much easier to check and adjust this now than after the leather has been glued on. Using a slightly diluted PVA (1:10 water to glue), glue the leather onto the base, leaving a fair margin to trim off with a sharp knife.

Cut the groove for the tray support. Again, as with the bottom groove, make sure that it doesn't show on the ends; it must either be a stopped groove or emerge in a tail. Position the tray support 48mm ($1^7/_8$in) from the top of the box (45mm ($1^3/_4$in) for the tray plus 3mm ($^1/_8$in) to allow for final sanding and a step down to the top of the tray). Sand the support piece to 400 grit and check for fit. If it's fractionally tight, it is easier to increase the groove by a whisker than to attempt to plane a whisker off the support.

Gluing up

Before gluing, sand all the inside faces to 400 grit. Clamp the box up using four sash clamps and substantial wooden blocks and immediately check for square using a squaring rod or rule across the diagonals. If the diagonals are not equal, reposition the clamps slightly as shown in Fig 9.4. I used a fifth clamp for this box just to make sure the sides were pulled tight against the shoulder of the center bar.

Fig 9.6 *Cutting the tenons on the base support using a radial saw with a stop clamped to the fence…*

Fig 9.7 *… Alternatively, the tenons can be marked out and cut with a backsaw and chisel*

Fig 9.8 *The plan of the base. It's sometimes easier to plane the plywood with a shallow chamfer so that it finishes at 5mm ($^3/_{64}$in) with the leather stuck on*

Fig 9.9 *Plywood can easily be cut to length by cutting through the two outside veneers with a knife*

Fig 9.10 *Trimming the leather*

Fig 9.11 *The groove for the tray support is routed before the box is assembled – if it emerges in a tail it need not be stopped*

Fig 9.12 *Section through tray and tray support*

Fig 9.13 *Any rectangle can be checked for square by measuring the diagonals*

Fig 9.14 *Slight corrections can be made to pull the box into square, using the sash clamps*

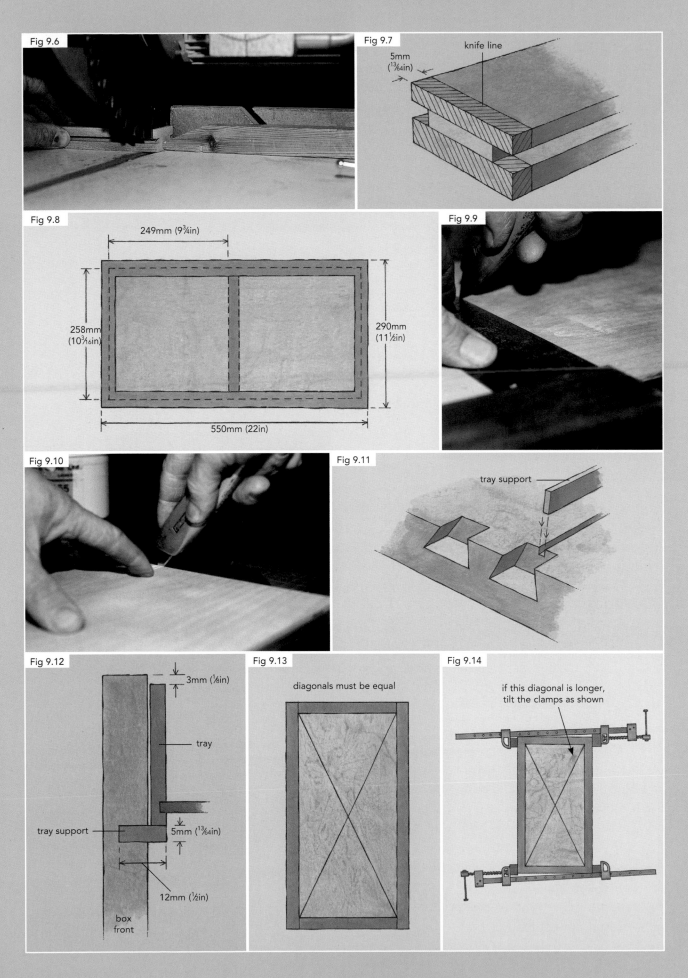

Fig 9.6

Fig 9.7

5mm
($\frac{13}{64}$in)

knife line

Fig 9.8

249mm (9$\frac{3}{4}$in)

258mm
(10$\frac{3}{16}$in)

290mm
(11$\frac{1}{2}$in)

550mm (22in)

Fig 9.9

Fig 9.10

Fig 9.11

tray support

Fig 9.12

3mm ($\frac{1}{8}$in)

tray

tray support

5mm ($\frac{13}{64}$in)

12mm ($\frac{1}{2}$in)

box
front

Fig 9.13

diagonals must be equal

Fig 9.14

if this diagonal is longer,
tilt the clamps as shown

The hinges

Back now to the strip of wood on which you scribbled 'hinges' and which was put to one side. First select where the knuckles will be. This section needs to be fairly straight- and even-grained so avoid burry bits, wild or sloping grain. Aim to have the knuckle just over one-third of the total length from the end, i.e. 270mm (10½in). Mark a rough line to indicate its position.

Mark the position of the hinges as in Fig 9.15 and use this side as the face side. Set a marking gauge to exactly half the thickness of the hinge and score a line on both edges 40–50mm (1½–2in) either side of the knuckle.

The pivot holes

For drilling the pivot holes there is no doubt that it is easier to use a machine vise on a drill table, but if you don't have this equipment, you can achieve the same result using a power or hand drill, with the work held in a vise.

Use a 5mm (¼in) lip-and-spur bit to drill very carefully through the width of the hinge, keeping the drill absolutely parallel to its face. The moment of truth will arrive when you check the exit hole – if it has come out exactly on the scribed line, congratulate yourself on a difficult job well done. If not, turn the hinge back over, move along 20mm (¾in) and try again. Even using a drill press and machine vise it is sometimes necessary to tilt the vise in order to get the hole parallel.

Drilling a hole parallel to the edge of a piece of wood can be achieved by coming at the problem from the opposite direction – drill the holes as carefully as possible and then, by careful planing, make the wood parallel to the hole.

Once you have achieved two good holes, separate the two hinge pieces and shoot or sand the ends so that they are parallel to the hole. I use my sanding disc and a home-made jig (my end-squaring-off-parallel-to-the-hole jig) for this job. (See hinge-making jigs in Chapter 2, p 16.)

The knuckles

An inverted router certainly earns its keep for cutting the slots in the knuckles, but the job can also be done by carefully marking out the slots, cutting with a backsaw and removing the waste using a coping saw and chisel.

Using the router, with the hinge clamped upright against the supplementary fence and waste wood behind it, cut the first slot to the pencil marks, ie 10mm (⅜in) from the edge. Hold this slot in position with a pin to cut the next slot, and follow this procedure for each subsequent slot. (See Figs 9.18, 9.19, 9.21 and 9.22.) Follow the same procedure for the rest of the hinge pieces, remembering that the

Fig 9.15 *Mark the hinges so you know which piece goes with which*

Fig 9.16 *Drilling the hinge pieces for the pivot*

Fig 9.17 *The hole doesn't always emerge exactly on the centerline*

Fig 9.18 *Plan view of the hinge-cutting jig*

Fig 9.19 *Exploded view of the hinge-cutting jig*

Fig 9.20 *The knuckles need to be just longer than the hinge is thick*

Fig 9.21 *Routing the first slot*

Fig 9.22 *Once the first slot has been routed, all the remaining slots are routed with the hinge located on a bolt screwed into a false fence*

Fig 9.23 *On the back hinge pieces, the end knuckles are sawn off and chiseled flat*

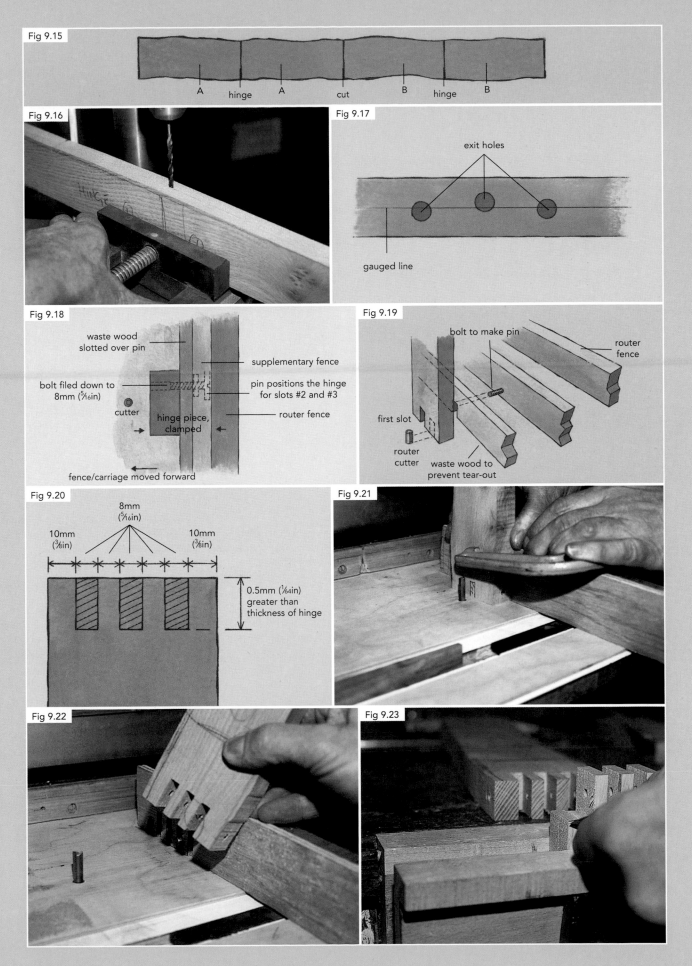

Fig 9.15
A   hinge   A   cut   B   hinge   B

Fig 9.16

Fig 9.17
exit holes
gauged line

Fig 9.18
waste wood
slotted over pin
supplementary fence
bolt filed down to
8mm (⁵⁄₁₆in)
pin positions the hinge
for slots #2 and #3
cutter
hinge piece,
clamped
router fence
fence/carriage moved forward

Fig 9.19
bolt to make pin
router
fence
first slot
router
cutter
waste wood to
prevent tear-out

Fig 9.20
8mm
(⁵⁄₁₆in)
10mm
(³⁄₈in)
10mm
(³⁄₈in)
0.5mm (¹⁄₆₄in)
greater than
thickness of hinge

Fig 9.21

Fig 9.22

Fig 9.23

center of this piece is a pin and not a slot. I forget exactly how many times I've cut two halves the same – this is a little annoying. There will be a larger pin left on either side of the hinge and these need finishing with a chisel.

Round the knuckles by first chiseling and then carefully sanding with a wooden block – do not use a cork block as the edges need to be kept straight and sharp. If you put much pressure on a cork block, it will try to take up the shape of the object it is being pressed on to.

If you are using a sanding disc it's fairly easy to construct a jig for this job. Build a 'stop' into each hinge by only partially radiusing the back part of each.

Positioning the hinges

It doesn't matter if the hinges are a bit stiff at this stage, as long as they slide into one another.

Cut the lid roughly to size, allowing about 6mm ($\frac{1}{4}$in) overhang on the sides and at the front. I usually form some sort of handle on my lids, always bearing in mind the natural shapes and forms of the figure.

At this point the hinges are still square. Place each hinge on the box lid and roughly outline their shape, following the grain pattern if possible and tapering them slightly towards the front. Keep them straight, curve them, or bend them towards the center. Cut the hinges to shape and size using a coping saw or band saw.

Position the hinges on the box, using a rod to connect them. (I used a rod of silver steel.) For this box, 60–70mm (about 2$\frac{1}{2}$in) in from the edge of the lid was about right. Check that the backs and tops of the hinges lie completely flat on the back and lid of the box. If the lid has even the slightest 'cap' in it, you must plane it flat. If the hinges don't lie flat with the rod connecting them, plane the underside of each until they do. Depending on how accurately the hinges have been made, this process can be long and drawn out. I have sometimes spent hours and hours taking hinges on and off a box.

Fixing the hinges

Mark the position of the pegs on the hinges with a scribbled circle. I find that four on the top and three at the back is usually sufficient. With a 10mm ($\frac{3}{8}$in) lip-and-spur bit, drill to within 4mm ($\frac{5}{32}$in) of the bottom of the hinge. It's a good idea to drill a test hole on the edge of a piece of waste, using a round-head screw ($\frac{5}{8}$in, No. 7) to check that when it's screwed up tight, it won't come through the bottom of the lid.

Reassemble the hinges on their rod and, using a small blob of PVA glue, press them onto the lid and back. Set the box to one side for the glue to dry. This is not a very strong glue joint (particularly on the back) and it's not meant to be. The glue simply holds the hinge in position while you drill the pilot holes for the screws.

Fig 9.24 *Rounding-off jig for knuckle of hinge*

Fig 9.25 *The knuckles are rounded either by careful sanding or using a jig attached to the sanding disc (see also Figs 2.25 and 2.26)*

Fig 9.26 *Only half of the back hinge piece is radiused; the rear half is left square to form a stop to keep the lid in an upright position*

Fig 9.27 *I think the hinges look better, happier somehow, if they're angled slightly inwards*

Fig 9.28 *Draw shapes onto the hinges until you're happy with the appearance and balance*

Fig 9.29 *A steel rod ensures that the hinge pivots are in line*

Fig 9.30 *The pegs are spaced out along the length of the hinge*

Fig 9.31 *Before drilling the peg hole in the hinges, use a piece of waste to check that there is no chance of the screw coming through to the other side of the lid*

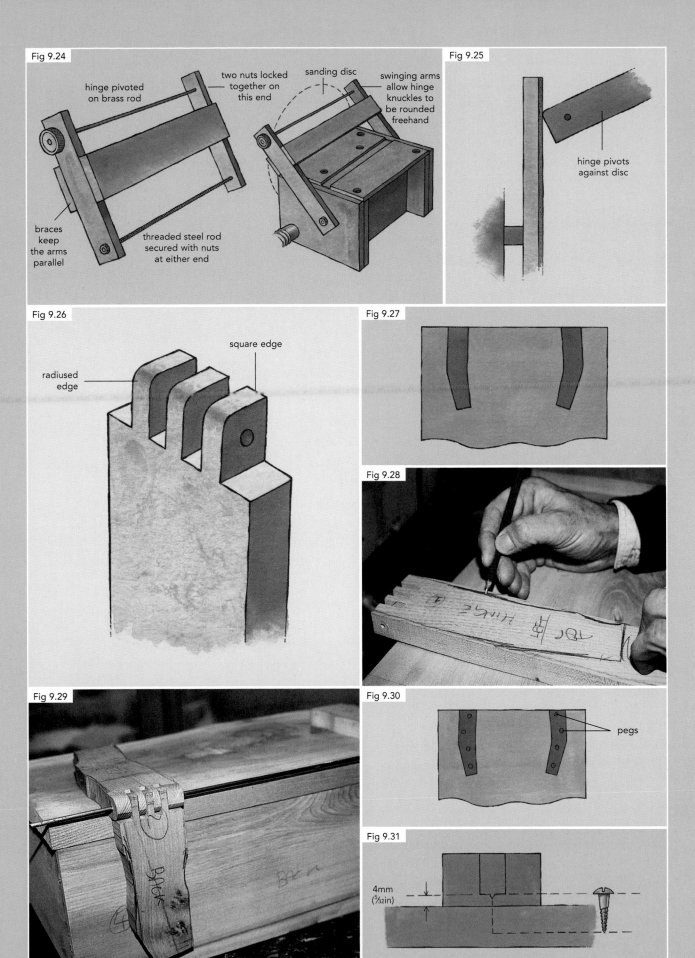

Fig 9.24

hinge pivoted on brass rod

two nuts locked together on this end

sanding disc

swinging arms allow hinge knuckles to be rounded freehand

braces keep the arms parallel

threaded steel rod secured with nuts at either end

Fig 9.25

hinge pivots against disc

Fig 9.26

radiused edge

square edge

Fig 9.27

Fig 9.28

Fig 9.29

Fig 9.30

pegs

Fig 9.31

4mm (5⁄32in)

Drill the pilot hole – 3mm (¹/₈in) in diameter – locating the drill bit in the V at the bottom of the 10mm (³/₈in) hole. A depth stop (a length of dowel in my case) is a very good idea. Drill bits appearing through the underside of the lid at this stage are not funny.

Don't be tempted to lift the lid. The glue will probably hold but it might not. Wait until you have drilled all of the pilot holes. All being well the lid should pivot perfectly and stop just beyond the vertical. Make sure the lid stops sufficiently far back that it won't slam shut on someone's fingers. Also check that each of the stops is doing its job. The best way to do this is to position the box in front of a good light (I use a window) and look through the hinges. The light will shine through any slight gaps, which can be cured by careful paring.

Trace around the back and top of each hinge in pencil, then prise them off with a broad chisel. Clean off any traces of glue using a scraper or an upright, 1in chisel.

Shaping

It is now time to shape the lid and box. I usually use an Arbortech or files and surforms, working with the grain pattern and softening the edges. If there are any defects, emphasize them. Overall, it's a good idea to achieve a slight convex shape on the sides of the box. I like the effect this has. It softens the overall shape and thins the top edge, making the whole thing appear lighter, while maintaining the strength of thicker material.

On the back and lid, take care not to cross the lines which were drawn around the hinges; carve down and away from these. This will leave the lid visually lighter by showing a thinner edge at the front. Bearing in mind the size of this box, the thickness at the edge of the lid should be around 16–17mm (¹¹/₁₆in).

Finishing

Your box should finally be taking shape and beginning to look worth all the trouble. Fit the tray supports by cutting them exactly to length and pushing them home with a little glue.

Shape the knuckles of the hinges and sand them to 400 grit – it won't be possible to get at these later.

Push a piece of dowel in from either side of the hinge and glue these in place with a drop or two of superglue, leaving a gap of about 1mm (¹/₃₂in) in the center. This gap means that no matter how the hinge decides to move in future years, whether it expands or contracts, the ends of the dowel will always remain flush. Use only the tiniest amount of glue. Capillary action will draw it into the hinge and the idea is that it goes no further than the first pin.

Sand the entire box to 180 grit and, with the lid in position, check that the overhang is equal on both sides. Sand the edges and ends of the hinges to 400 grit, then trace around them in pencil again, lightly,

Fig 9.32 *Once the hinges are glued in position, use a piece of dowel as a stop and drill pilot holes*

Fig 9.33 *The drill bit runs through a piece of dowel which acts as a stop*

Fig 9.34 *Before gluing the pivots in place, check that the hinge stops in the correct position*

Fig 9.35 *The lid is stopped about 10° from vertical*

Fig 9.36 *Paring the hinge stops*

Fig 9.37 *Once the pilot holes are drilled, the hinges can be levered off using a broad chisel*

Fig 9.38 *Shaping the box*

Fig 9.39 *Front view of the box showing how the lid is shaped*

Fig 9.40 *Inserting the tray support*

Fig 9.41 *The desired final shape for the knuckles*

Fig 9.42 *The knuckles are shaped before the pivots are glued in*

Fig 9.43 *One or, at most, two drops of superglue will secure the pivot*

Fig 9.44 *Leave a gap between the pivots in the center of the hinge*

Fig 9.45 *Sanding the lid*

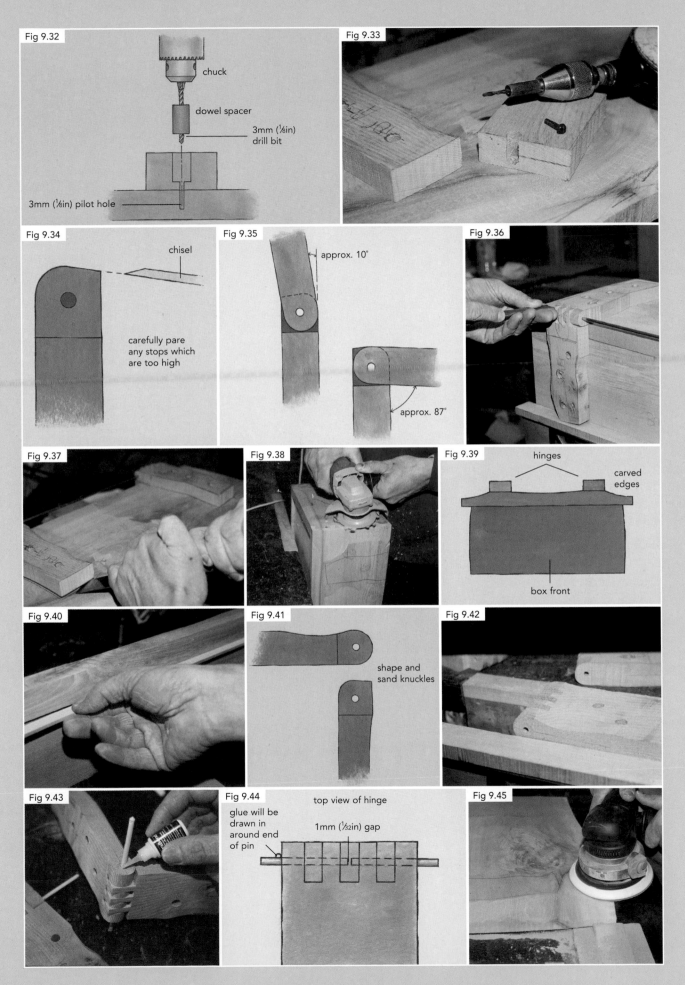

Fig 9.32

chuck

dowel spacer

3mm (⅛in)
drill bit

3mm (⅛in) pilot hole

Fig 9.33

Fig 9.34

chisel

carefully pare
any stops which
are too high

Fig 9.35

approx. 10°

approx. 87°

Fig 9.36

Fig 9.37

Fig 9.38

Fig 9.39

hinges

carved
edges

box front

Fig 9.40

Fig 9.41

shape and
sand knuckles

Fig 9.42

Fig 9.43

glue will be
drawn in
around end
of pin

Fig 9.44

top view of hinge

1mm (½in) gap

Fig 9.45

to mark their outline on the boxes. Now finish sanding the entire box, working up to the pencil outline of the hinges until it just disappears.

Sand the bottom edges, checking the box on a piece of glass or other flat surface, then take off the sharp outside edges using a cork block, and the sharp inside edges with the sandpaper held in your hand. When you are working on the inside, use a piece of plywood or heavy card to protect the sanded base.

Now sand the entire box and lid with a final grit of 400.

Final hinge fitting

The hinges can now be fitted permanently. Enlarge the 3mm ($^1/_8$in) screw holes to 5mm ($^{13}/_{64}$in) so that the lid can expand or contract independently of the hinge.

Fix each hinge piece in place, using only two screws at first, and check for opening and stopping one final time. Check the back of the lid to make sure it doesn't bind on the back of the box or the back of the hinge. There should be a gap of about 1mm ($^1/_{32}$in). If everything works to plan, the hinges can now be screwed into place.

Shape the ends of the hinges so that they taper from the back, finishing at about 12mm ($^1/_2$in). Take off all sharp edges and finish sanding to 400 grit.

To make the pegs, cut a piece of leftover wood to a 10.5mm ($^{13}/_{32}$in) square section, about 200mm (10in) long. I sometimes use contrasting wood for pegs. Holding this wood in the vise, across its diagonals, plane the square to an octagon. Next, holding it flat on the bench, put a taper on the end of the peg, using the tip of a chisel, and saw off about 15mm ($^5/_8$in). Put a little PVA glue in each hole and tap the pegs home.

Using a sharp chisel bevel-side down, cut each dowel off at about 2mm ($^5/_{64}$in) above the hinge taking four upward cuts to leave the dowels finished with four facets.

Finishing

Finish the box with two or three coats of Danish oil, leave it to dry completely, then give it a final coat of beeswax.

Fig 9.46 *Use a piece of 1.5mm (¹⁄₁₆in) plywood to protect the sanded base when taking the sharp edge off the bottom inside edge*

Fig 9.47 *Check that all of the stops are working together*

Fig 9.48 *Check that there is a gap of about 1mm (¹⁄₃₂in) under the lid at the back, and enlarge the 3mm (¹⁄₈in) pilot hole in the hinge to 5mm (¹³⁄₆₄in)*

Fig 9.49 *If the stops are not all acting together, they might need paring slightly*

Fig 9.50 *Once the hinge is fixed in position, it can be shaped by tapering it slightly towards the front*

Fig 9.51 *A piece of 10.5mm (¹³⁄₃₂in) square-section material is planed to an octagon*

Fig 9.52 *The corners are taken off the octagonal section*

Fig 9.53 *The pegs are faceted using a sharp, bevel-edged chisel*

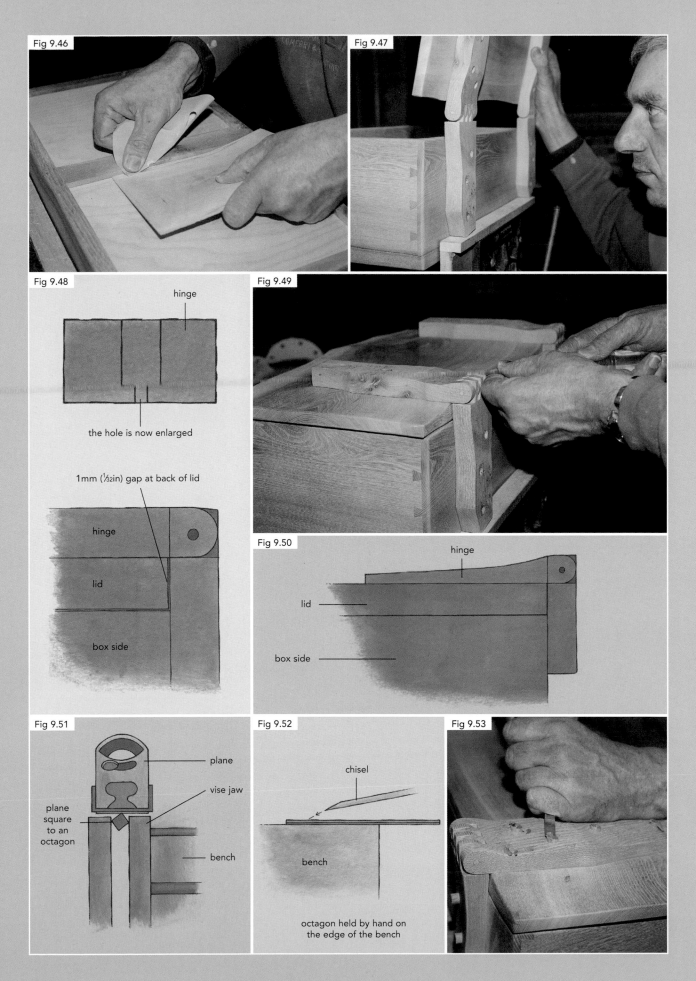

Fig 9.46

Fig 9.47

Fig 9.48

hinge

the hole is now enlarged

1mm (½2in) gap at back of lid

hinge

lid

box side

Fig 9.49

Fig 9.50

hinge

lid

box side

Fig 9.51

plane

vise jaw

plane
square
to an
octagon

bench

Fig 9.52

chisel

bench

octagon held by hand on
the edge of the bench

Fig 9.53

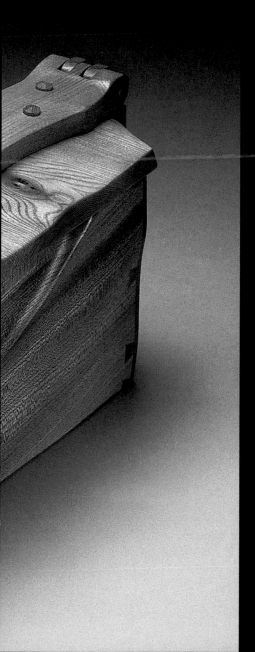

STATIONERY BOX

W hen I first thought about making a box with a drawer, I didn't much like the idea. Drawers, I knew, were not easy. Was I up to it? However, the customer said drawer so drawer it had to be. And I'd said yes. I seldom say no, which can make for an interesting life; it certainly stretches the old gray matter.

I decided that I didn't want to impose the drawer onto the box; I wanted the drawer to be a part of the box and a part of the wood as well. I wanted it to sit happily with the figure of the wood and not slash across it. So it had to be curved and it had to be cut from the same material.

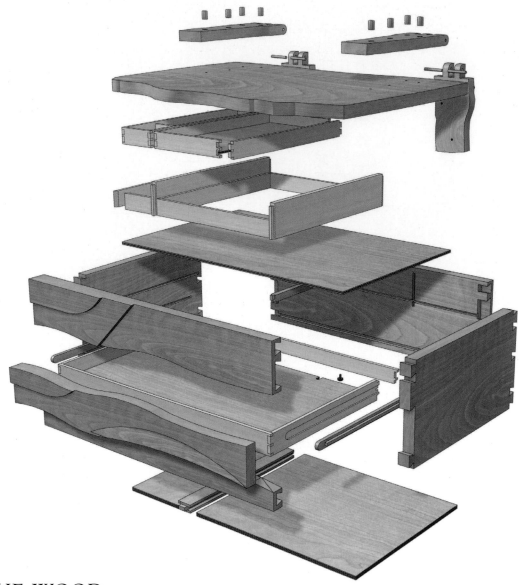

THE WOOD

I chose burr elm for this stationery box. It is available in wide boards, and the piece I chose provided the perfect front – 50mm (2in) or so of burry edge giving way to swirling figure that I could use for the drawer.

THE PROCESS

Choose a board for this box bearing in mind the same criteria as for the work box (see Chapter 9, p 92). As the lid for this box is much wider, however, it's even more important that the wood is completely dry and stable (see Chapter 1, p 4). Of course, stable is a relative term: any wood with burr in it may behave unpredictably and could well have built-up internal stresses which may not become apparent until after the wood has been cut. It's a good idea to let the wood acclimatize for a few weeks once the drawer has been cut so that any stresses in the front have a chance to settle down. Far better to find out at this stage – as I did with my box – that the drawer is going to bow and twist out of shape.

Map out the four sides of the box choosing the front piece, from which the drawer will be cut, very carefully. With regard to wood movement, the drawer is probably the most critical part of this box so I tend to choose a piece which is not too burry and wild at the bottom but with a little burr at the top to connect the front of the box to the lid visually.

Once the box has been mapped out (including the hinges), number the sides and cut each piece precisely to length and width. Note that the front is 10mm (³⁄₈in) wider than the back and sides.

The drawer front

Now mark the drawer onto the front using long, sweeping curves either to take up the figure in the wood or to contrast with it. The drawer should be the same height at either end. I have found that a power jigsaw gives a good clean cut but a band saw or bow saw would do just as well. Whatever type of saw you use, make sure the blade cuts along the curve in one long, fluid movement. If the saw drifts off the line, ease it back on course gradually. At all costs, avoid sudden kinks in the cut. As I mentioned earlier, if at all possible, leave the box for a couple of weeks at this stage. Once your wood has had a chance to acclimatize, clean off the saw marks from the four edges, removing as little as possible. I find the best way of doing this is to fold and hold down some sandpaper with your thumb. If the wood has moved, more drastic measures might be necessary – you may need a spokeshave or surform. With the saw marks removed, check for high spots by holding the pieces up against the light or in front of a window. The idea is to get as near perfect a fit as possible but, unless the saw cut was very clean and the wood very stable, a perfect fit is not that easy to achieve; there is always a chink of light coming through somewhere. (See Fig 10.3.)

Fig 10.1 *The drawer is marked onto the front of the box*

Fig 10.2 *Sanding the drawer edge*

Fig 10.3 *Checking that the drawer has a close fit*

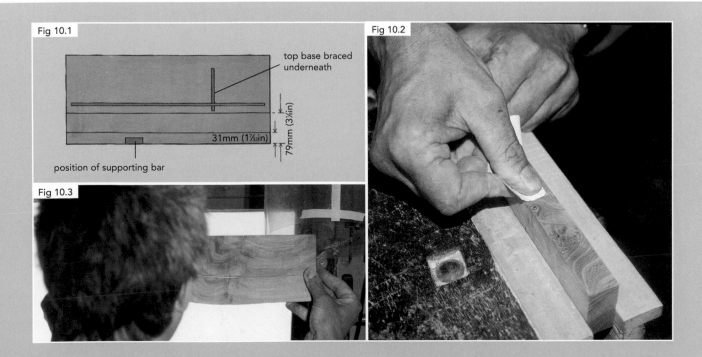

Fig 10.1

top base braced
underneath

position of supporting bar

31mm (1¼in)

79mm (3⅛in)

Fig 10.2

Fig 10.3

With the drawer front fitting as tightly as possible and the sides lined up, use masking tape on both sides to tape it in position. You can now treat the front of the box as one piece of wood. Plane it to the same width as the sides and back, assuming that the 10mm ($^3/_8$in) extra allowed on the front was enough for the saw cuts and finishing (see Fig 10.4). If it wasn't, you will have to reduce the back and sides to match the front.

The dovetails

Leaving the front taped in position, map and cut out the dovetails. I spaced my dovetails so that they were the same on the back and front of the box, cutting one large dovetail on the back to the height of the drawer (see Fig 10.5). There is no dovetail cut into the drawer front.

Assemble the box and check that it stands flat and level, using a machine table or a piece of glass, and that there are no steps between the pieces. If necessary, gently remove any high spots. It is best to use a try plane for this as the sole of the plane can rest on both edges. The top edge can be left as it is at this stage.

The base

The next step is to cut the plywood for the base of the box, using two pieces with a supporting bar in the same way as described for the work box (see Chapter 9, p 93). Position the support to coincide with one of the upward curves in the drawer front (see Fig 10.7).

Now cut the plywood base for the top section of the box. This can be made in one piece and will be supported by a divider. Cover both sides of the plywood in leather and measure the resultant thickness, preferably with a pair of calipers. Select a cutter for the router. If you don't have one of the correct size for the base, use the next size down and cut the grooves for the top and bottom bases in two passes.

Using the same cutter, rout a stopped groove on both sides of the box to take the drawer runners. This groove should be around 5mm ($^{13}/_{64}$in) wide but it doesn't have to be exact as the drawer runners will be rabbeted to match the groove later.

The dividers

Next, cut the vertical grooves for the dividing pieces. These should be around 4mm ($^5/_{32}$in) wide but again, use whatever cutters are closest to this size as the dividers will be cut later, to suit the grooves. What does need to be accurate is the position of the grooves or the envelopes and paper won't fit. It doesn't really matter whether the narrow division for the pens is on the left or the right of the box but one of the dividers needs to run through the base groove so that the top base can be braced underneath; position them so that the curve of the drawer front allows for the largest possible brace.

Fig 10.4 *Use masking tape to re-join the drawer front to the box front*

Fig 10.5 *The box side, showing the spacing of the dovetails*

Fig 10.6 *Use a try plane to make the base flat*

Fig 10.7 *The inside of the box, showing the support bar*

Fig 10.8 *The groove for the drawer runners is stopped*

Fig 10.9 *Cutting one of the dividers in two*

Fig 10.10 *Removing the end of the tenon with a chisel*

To find the length required for the dividing pieces, measure the distance between the shoulders of an end piece, add the depth of both grooves and subtract 1mm ($^1/_{32}$in). For my box the equation was $255 + 14 - 1 = 268$mm ($10 + ^9/_{16} + ^1/_{32} = 10^{19}/_{32}$in). Cut the dividing pieces to length, then cut the shoulders on them. I used a pair of slotting cutters in the inverted router for this job but a radial arm saw or a single straight router cutter could be used equally well. On the divider that is to go above and below the top base, it is best to cut the shoulders before cutting it into two: it is much easier to cut both shoulders on a wide piece of wood than cut the first on a wide piece and the second on a narrow one. Carefully pare the top of the tenon down to the shoulders with a chisel.

Fig 10.4

Fig 10.5

dovetail pins are all equal size

drawer

side

Fig 10.6

Fig 10.7

Fig 10.8

Fig 10.9

Fig 10.10

Now cut the drawer runners from the 8mm (⁵/₁₆in) sycamore, using a router to cut the rabbet and remove the tongue at either end. Sand all the inside faces of the box, both sides and one edge of the dividers, both sides and both edges of the bottom support to 400 grit. The end grain of the edge where the drawer slots in must also be sanded, but take care not to overdo this: the dovetails won't fit if too much material is removed and the drawer will not close neatly. I use abrasive wrapped around a dovetail-shaped wooden block for this.

It's a good idea to take the sharp edge off the grooves for the top and bottom base at this stage. This will help the leather-covered plywood slip into its groove. Also, if you gently hammer the edge of the leather on a flat surface, it is much less likely to ruck up on the grooves when the box is being assembled.

Before gluing up, assemble and clamp the box dry. Check that the shoulders of the dividers are tight against the front and back when the sash clamps are tight. If they need a clamp to keep them tight, they are probably too loose. It is far preferable to have these slightly long and keeping the front and back apart than to cut them too short and have trouble keeping them together. There is any amount of compression strength in these pieces but the joints on the ends are really only to locate them. If they were under tension they would very quickly spring apart.

Gluing up

Once everything has been checked on a dry run take a deep breath, put up the 'do not disturb' signs and get out the glue pot. Assemble the back and front first, with the dividers and base in place, and then, taking care not to spread too much glue on the surfaces where it can squeeze out, assemble the sides. It would be impossible to get rid of glue from the drawer space after this step. Make sure the pressure is applied square to the joint as you tighten the sash clamps.

The drawer frame

It is time now to start work on the drawer frame. Making the frame separate from the drawer front is not the traditional way of making a drawer, but this isn't a traditional box and for me it's the best method. I suppose if I extended that argument the drawer could be made the same width all the way around and a plywood base could be let in to stopped grooves, in much the same way as I make my trays (see trays in Chapter 3, p 28). This would be marginally easier but, to me, it somehow seems more 'right' to make the drawer with the base fixed onto the underside of the drawer back. Make the length of the drawer front exactly the same as the width of the opening. This should give about a 2mm (⁵/₆₄in) clearance once the drawer is glued up. Make the side about 5mm (¹³/₆₄in) shorter than the available space. This should make a drawer that accepts A4 paper (297 × 210mm/11¾ × 8¼in) neatly and allows a finger to remove it.

Fig 10.11 *The drawer runners are chiselled flat at the ends*

Fig 10.12 *This small wooden block is used to sand the end grain against which the drawer stops*

Fig 10.13 *Using the block illustrated in Fig 10.12*

Fig 10.14 *Taking the sharp edge off the grooves*

Fig 10.15 *Hammering the edge of the leather will thin it out slightly*

Fig 10.16 *All clamped up*

Fig 10.11
tongue removed
at both ends
drawer runner

Fig 10.12
abrasive wrapped around a dovetail-shaped wooden block

Fig 10.13

Fig 10.14

Fig 10.15

Fig 10.16

Dovetail the drawer frame using through dovetails at the back and front. I prefer to cut the tails first and then mark these onto the pins. Check that the frame is level on the underside and, if necessary, remove any steps between pieces, then rout a groove for the drawer base. Once again I used plywood which was covered with leather on both sides but covering just one side would be perfectly adequate. Put the drawer to one side now and return to the box.

Carving and shaping

Slot the drawer front into place and wedge it into position by wrapping some masking tape around it. Following the figure in the wood and the shape of the drawer, pencil two sweeping curves on the front of the box. These will be carved and deepened to form handles where they cross the drawer front so they should be about equidistant from the center of the drawer front. Think also of what the lid will look like when you pencil in these curves and where the handle will be. It wouldn't look right if the whole thing was unbalanced by too much happening on one side.

An Arbortech certainly makes short work of carving the front. Keep the curves flowing smoothly and undercut the drawer handles very gently, a little at a time. It wouldn't be totally disastrous to cut the drawer front right through to the other side but I think on this box it is better not.

Getting the drawer handles smooth and even is a job that simply needs bucket loads of patience. A burr cutter in a flexible drive will be an enormous help but in the end it comes down to abrasive paper and elbow grease. A little device that I have found useful for this job is a piece of dowel about 75mm (3in) long, 8mm ($^5/_{16}$in) in diameter and with a saw cut at one end. I insert a piece of good cloth-backed abrasive into the slot, wrap the rest around the dowel and then, holding the abrasive-covered dowel, push it into the power-drill chuck. The abrasive does wear out and tear pretty quickly but it's a device that is well worth making. The drawer front doesn't need to be finished at this stage. If the curves are good and the drawer pulls are sufficiently undercut, sand the front to about 60 grit, then put it to one side.

Back to the drawer now. With the front of the drawer frame laid on the back of the drawer front, the best positions for the screws can be seen. It's important to keep the screws well away from the drawer pulls as it is around these that the front is at its thinnest, so there is a risk of the screw emerging from the other side – not a pretty sight. Use a pair of calipers to check this. Once the rough positions have been established, measure, mark, drill and counterbore these holes with a 7mm ($^9/_{32}$in) bit. In order to get them evenly spaced, you will have to compromise with their positions.

You can now sand the inside faces of the drawer frame and glue the frame up. My dovetails are seldom so perfect that they don't need

Fig 10.17 *Dovetails on the sides of the drawer frame*

Fig 10.18 *Marking around the dovetails onto the pins*

Fig 10.19 *Cutting the waste from between the pins*

Fig 10.20 *Removing the waste using a coping saw*

Fig 10.21 *Chisel to the knife line square across but either chisel only to the center, or have a piece of waste wood clamped to the back of the drawer piece*

Fig 10.22 *The back of the drawer*

Fig 10.23 *Roughly marking the lines for the drawer handles*

Fig 10.24 *My sanding device – a length of abrasive-covered dowel*

Fig 10.25 *A small burr cutter that I use for undercutting the handles*

Fig 10.26 *Using calipers to check the positions for the screws*

Fig 10.27 *Strictly speaking, dovetails shouldn't be clamped at all – they should be tapped home and the pins slightly burred over to hold them in position while the glue dries. Would that mine were that perfect! I do clamp mine but it is important that the clamp applies pressure square to the joint*

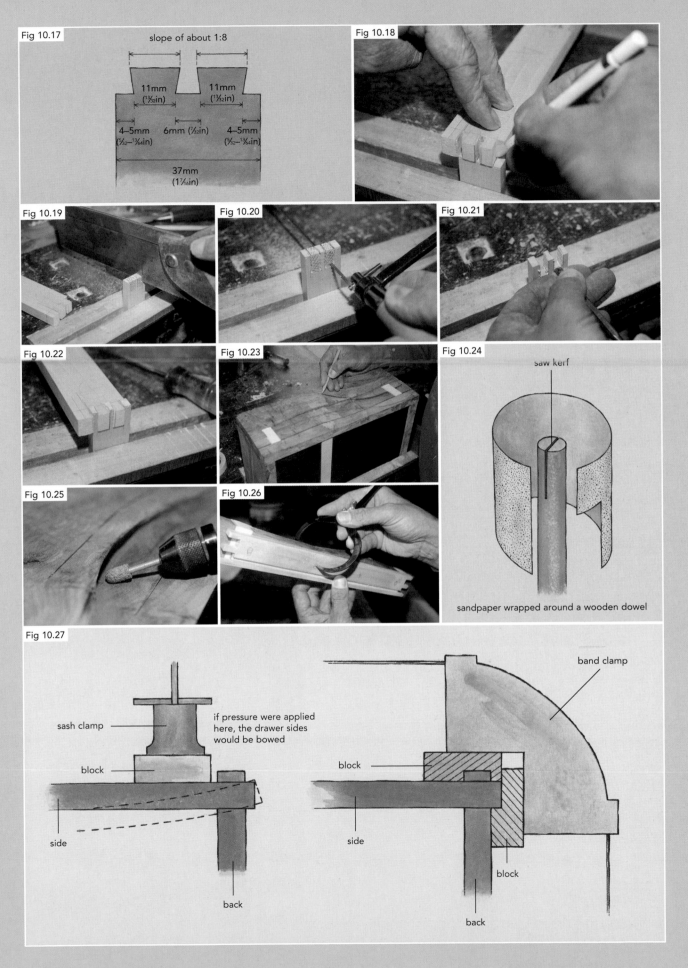

Fig 10.17

slope of about 1:8

11mm (¹³⁄₃₂in) 11mm (¹³⁄₃₂in)

4–5mm (⁵⁄₃₂–¹³⁄₆₄in) 6mm (⁷⁄₃₂in) 4–5mm (⁵⁄₃₂–¹³⁄₆₄in)

37mm (1⁷⁄₁₆in)

Fig 10.18

Fig 10.19

Fig 10.20

Fig 10.21

Fig 10.22

Fig 10.23

Fig 10.24

saw kerf

sandpaper wrapped around a wooden dowel

Fig 10.25

Fig 10.26

Fig 10.27

sash clamp

if pressure were applied here, the drawer sides would be bowed

block

side

back

band clamp

block

block

side

back

113

clamping and with the pins and tails projecting about 1mm ($^1/_{32}$in),
I was faced with the task of clamping the frame up without throwing
it out of shape – just what might happen if I used sash clamps. I
over-came this by cutting a piece of 5mm ($^{13}/_{64}$in) sycamore into strips
of different widths and using a drop of PVA to glue them over the
dovetails and pins. Then, using eight blocks to spread the pressure,
I clamped the frame using a band clamp. If you can't get your hands
on a band clamp, use two lengths of string; wind one around the top
of the frame several times, and the other around the bottom. Tighten
these lengths of string by twisting them with wooden levers, using one
on each side, one on the front and one on the back of the box – eight
in total. Again, at the risk of repeating myself, it is essential to have a
dry run before gluing the frame for real.

The hinges

With the drawer frame glued, clamped up and put to one side, the
hinges can be made. Follow the same method as for the hinges of the
work box (see Chapter 9, p 96).

The interior

The bearers for the trays are made from eight pieces of 35 × 5mm ($1^3/_8$ ×
$^{13}/_{64}$in) sycamore which sit inside the pen compartment and the central
compartment. These are mitered in position. I do this job in two stages.
First, I cut the sycamore to overall length, allowing plenty for waste.
I then mark it out, write an identification number on the back and sand
the front to 400 grit. Next I cut out the eight pieces, 2–3mm (approx.
$^1/_8$in) oversize, then cut a miter on one end of each. I use my miter block
and disc sander for this but a miter shooting board or a guillotine would
do just as well. Mark the front and back, left and right side of each
piece, making sure the joint (where the grain will not match) comes
at the front, then cut each piece precisely to the lines. The pen
compartment is subdivided into three. (See trays in Chapter 3, p 28.)

Trace around the hinges then prise them off with a broad chisel.
With reference to the figure of the wood, continue the curves on
the front of the box round to the sides. The lid, too, should have a
suggestion of a curved ridge but I don't like to overdo these things.

Refining the shape

Now it's back to work with the Arbortech to generally reduce the
thickness of the box sides and work up to the sweeping curves.
After the Arbortech, it's back to sandpaper. This is where a good
rotary sander pays for its keep but it isn't essential – elbow grease
and patience will work just as well. Sand the whole of the box, except
for the front, down to 240 grit. Leave the front at about
120 grit at this stage: it's best to finish sanding it once the drawer
has been properly fitted.

Fig 10.28 *A band clamp is useful for clamping up the frame*

Fig 10.29 *Detail of a joint, showing the temporary wooden strips*

Fig 10.30 *The hinges are held in line with a steel rod*

Fig 10.31 *Shaping the lid*

Fitting the drawer

You should now turn your attention back to the drawer. Lever off the
wooden blocks. I didn't apply pressure when these were glued on and

Fig 10.28

Fig 10.29

Fig 10.30

Fig 10.31

I found I could just push them off with my thumb. Carefully plane down the tails and pins, then check that the frame is absolutely flat, on a machine table or a piece of glass, taking a fine shaving off at any point if necessary.

Extend the centerlines of the drawer-runner grooves with a light pencil line and, with the drawer frame held in its opening, mark this centerline on the frame sides. These marks must be the same on either side.

Rout a stopped groove on either side of the drawer frame for the drawer runners. These grooves should be fractionally larger – about 0.3mm (^{1}/$_{64}$in) – than the runners. Now comes a moment of truth. If the runners weren't marked or cut out accurately the frame may touch the bottom or top tails. All is not lost if it does. This is the reason for not gluing the runners before the box is assembled. If the drawer frame needs moving up or down, new runners can be made. The runners should be made oversize and then planed so that there is as little side-to-side movement as possible. Round off the ends of the runners on the sanding disc.

Hammer two panel pins (brads) into the front of the frame (making sure they don't go right through) and snip them off with a pair of pincers. Then, using a block of scrap wood to prevent the frame from going all the way back into the box, push the drawer front onto the pins to mark the position for the screws. Remove the frame and, using just two screws at first, screw the frame onto the drawer front. Take off the masking tape that has been wedging the drawer in position all this time and the drawer should fit perfectly. Remove the pins, sand the frame and the drawer front to 400 grit, then glue and screw the drawer front into position. Counterbore and plug these screws in the same way as the hinges.

You can now sand the whole box down to 400 grit, then attach and finish the hinges in the same way as for the work box (see Chapter 9, p 98).

Cut the base of the drawer from 4mm (^{5}/$_{32}$in) plywood and cover it with leather as you did the box base. If you line it on one side only I suggest that you fix the base in place by screwing it to the back of the drawer frame. The traditional way of fixing drawer bases is by screwing them into a slot. This is to allow some movement of the base where solid wood is being used. Movement in plywood is virtually non-existent and a straightforward counter-sunk screw would do the job perfectly satisfactorily. I covered both sides of the drawer bottom with leather and while I could have used round-head screws to fix the bottom to the back of the frame I wanted to keep the box all wood so I asked a friend to turn me some wooden pegs.

This box has two trays: a pen tray and a compliments slip/envelope tray. Both are lined with leather. (See trays in Chapter 3, p 28.) To finish, give the box two or three coats of Danish oil and then wax.

Fig 10.32 *Marking the position of the drawer runner onto the drawer*

Fig 10.33 *Push the drawer front onto the frame to locate it, using the panel pins (brads)*

Fig 10.34 *The slot allows the drawer base to move within it, though with a plywood base it's not really necessary*

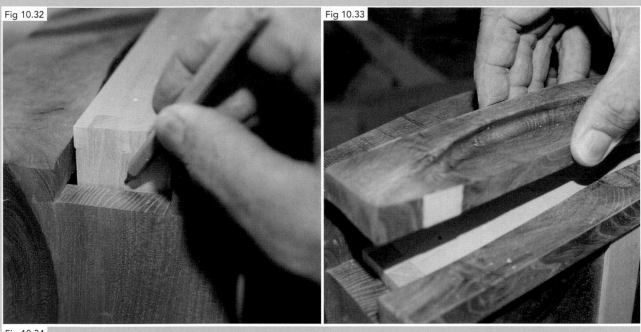

Fig 10.32

Fig 10.33

Fig 10.34

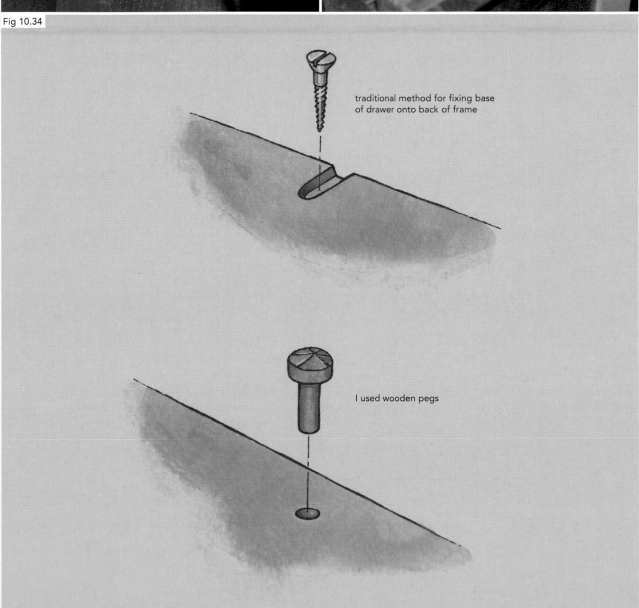

traditional method for fixing base
of drawer onto back of frame

I used wooden pegs

BACK HINGE

Back hinges were my answer to a wooden hinge that wasn't so 'in your face', that didn't shout at you, 'hey, I'm a hinge', as soon as you caught sight of it. I made big boxes with big chunky hinges, and for a quieter box I used brass hinges (which I used to get silver plated) with a chain for the lid stay. But the chain ran through brass guides which I had to make on a friend's metalworking lathe, and I wanted to do all the work in my own workshop. I didn't want to buy hinges and make do; I wanted to be in control. And I wanted hinges that added something to the box, not just be there. So I conceived a wooden hinge. Let into the back of the box it was unobtrusive, and without any extra messing about, it worked as a lid stay. I like both my strap hinges and my back hinges, but I do find that many people strongly prefer one over the other.

Jewelry box

p 121

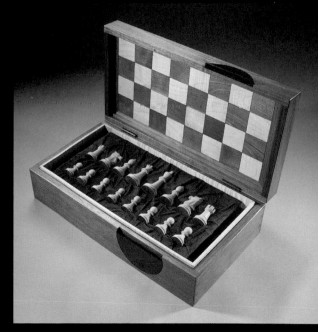

Chess box

p 135

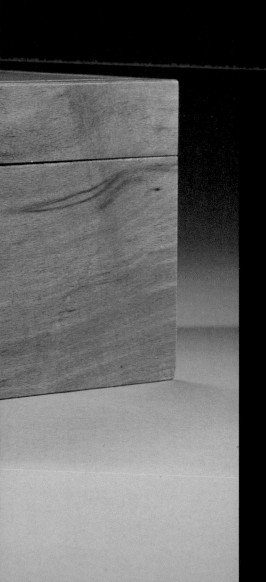

JEWELRY BOX

With this plank lying on the bench in front of me I was struck immediately by its pattern – in fact I think I even said out loud 'I like those flames'. The pattern was, of course, right in the middle of the plank which meant that the sides couldn't be marked out in an uninterrupted strip but nevertheless, the flames had to be on the lid. So, with a rectangle drawn around the flames, about lid size, I set about mapping the rest of the box onto the plank. In fact it turned out to be easier than I had feared and I ended up with a box 230 × 330 × 140mm (9 × 13$\frac{1}{4}$ × 5$\frac{1}{2}$in).

I planed the board to a thickness of 20mm ($\frac{3}{4}$in) and intended to put a slight curve on the sides and the lid with the Arbortech once the box was complete. However, when I saw the sides assembled on the bench I realized that even with the 'flamed' lid this box needed something extra. It was altogether too plain. This piece of beech was boring. It needed some oomph. Perhaps a handle or a catch on the front. I played around with various ideas and eventually settled for a disc of bog oak which would pick up some of the darker lines in the beech and make a stunning feature on the front of the box.

Somehow a circle didn't seem to sit happily alongside a free-formed, curved lid. A straighter, squarer, altogether more geometrical box was called for. So, with the sides reduced to 18mm ($\frac{11}{16}$in) and a rough pencil circle drawn on the front of the box, I was off on a new tack.

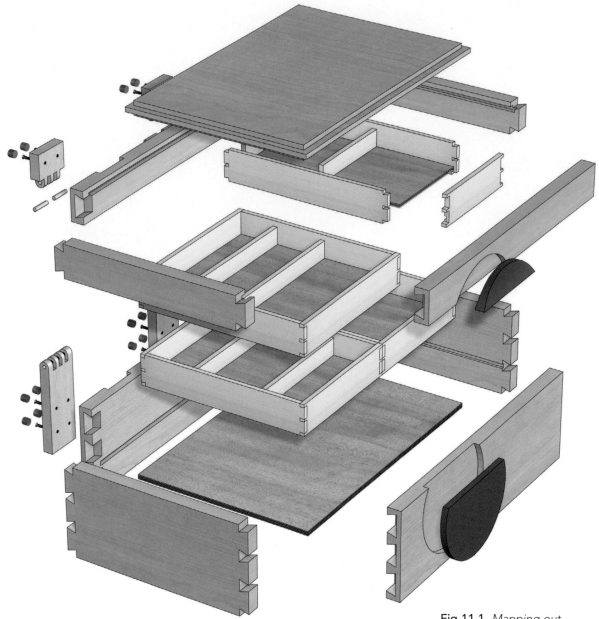

THE WOOD

Beech is a boring old wood which I associate with school desks (it is what they were made of before plastic-covered chipboard) and wooden spoons. It is sometimes a little flecked when it's been quarter-sawn, but is generally just plain boring. However, I had a piece that wasn't. It was flamed with dark lines and streaked with red.

I don't buy wood for a box; I buy wood that appeals to me, that is unusual in some way and that will look dramatic even in small pieces. Once I've bought it, it goes onto the shelf and either waits until the right box comes along or until I heave it onto the bench and think, now what sort of box will this make. This piece told me that it wanted to be a fairly restrained, formal and traditional sort of box. Nothing hobbit-like or wild, wacky and Walt Disney.

THE PROCESS

Cut the sides and ends to size and check that they are square and of identical lengths. Next, cut the lapped dovetails, allowing an extra 4mm (5/32in) on the pin where the lid will be cut off. Remove any steps, preferably with a try plane or at least a plane that's long enough always to be touching on two sides of the box, then check that the box is flat by putting it onto a machine table or a piece of glass.

Fig 11.1

Fig 11.2

Fig 11.3

Fig 11.4

Fig 11.5

Fig 11.6

With the dovetails pushed firmly home, measure the inside dimensions and add 12mm ($\frac{1}{2}$in) to find the size of the base and the lid. For the base, cut a piece of 4mm ($\frac{5}{32}$in) plywood to these dimensions and cover one side in moiré. Double-sided tape works well for this but at a pinch, a very thin coat of undiluted PVA will do the job. I must emphasize very thin and not in the least watered down: if it's too wet or too thick it will bleed through the fabric. Cut the lid piece to exactly the same size. Squareness is essential.

Now to the router. If the 4mm ($\frac{5}{32}$in) plywood base is, in fact, 4mm ($\frac{5}{32}$in), you will need to cut a groove of slightly over 4mm ($\frac{5}{32}$in). My plywood always seems to be a bit under 4mm ($\frac{5}{32}$in) so with the thickness of the moiré added, a 4mm ($\frac{5}{32}$in) straight cutter does the job. Rout the groove to a depth of 7mm ($\frac{9}{32}$in) to ensure that the base will not prevent the dovetails from coming up tightly when the box is glued up. The groove can run the full length of the ends but must be stopped on the front and back. Plane the lid to a thickness of 15mm ($\frac{19}{32}$in).

Reset the fence on the router, change the cutter to a 5mm ($\frac{13}{64}$in) straight cutter and rout a groove 6mm ($\frac{1}{4}$in) down from the top edge. This will give a 1mm ($\frac{1}{32}$in) lip to clean up once the lid is in position. Do not rout the groove with the top edge against the fence: for one thing the top was not leveled but, more importantly, working from the same edge all the time ensures that everything remains parallel.

The lid

Cut the lid to exactly the same size as the plywood base, i.e. 12mm ($\frac{1}{2}$in) larger than the inside measurements of the box. Then, using a router or a rabbet plane, form the tongue around the edge of the lid. Using a router does mean working from both sides, so it is crucial that the lid is of even thickness. A wedge-shaped lid will result in a wedge-shaped tongue.

The inside face of the lid and the inside faces of the sides and ends must now be sanded to 400 grit. With this done, the box is ready to glue up. It's a very good idea to do a dummy run on this job. It is one of life's immutable laws that if something is going to go wrong it will wait until the glue is on the joints before it does. With the clamps and blocks ready, quickly paint glue onto all the dovetails, slip the lid and base into their slots on the front and back and then, with a little glue about halfway along in the lid grooves, and taking care not to catch the moiré on the base, tap the end pieces home.

Gluing up

Before putting on the clamps, check the gap around the lid. Relying on your eye or using spacers, make sure the gap is even all the way around. I have some chopped plastic draft excluder which I use for this job. If the gap is not even and needs shifting slightly, rather than

Fig 11.7 *The plywood base is covered with moiré and trimmed*

Fig 11.8 *The tongue on the lid is cut on the router*

Fig 11.9 *A centerline is marked on the edge of the hinge*

putting a lever into it, tap the box sharply with a hammer on the side which the lid is to move towards. It doesn't sound logical but it works. Finally, clamp up the dovetails, heave a big sigh of relief and gratefully accept any offers of cups of tea.

The hinges

At least now the box is looking a bit more box-like but you must put it to one side because the next job is the hinges. For these you need two pieces of wood 15 × 52 × 170mm ($^{19}/_{32}$ × 2 × 7in). I used the same wood as the box – beech. A contrasting wood could be used but avoid too severe a contrast and consider using the second wood for the trays. I think too many different woods in one small box can start to look a bit messy. A length of 170mm (7in) may sound a bit long but I prefer to use a piece with plenty to spare.

The hinges for this box are made in a very similar way to the hinges for the work box (see Chapter 9, p 96). However, to save you flicking back and forth I will run through the method again. The main differences lie in the number and size of the knuckles and in the rounding off.

Mark the face side of these lengths of wood and from this side, use a marking gauge to gauge a line exactly halfway. Next, using a machine vise or drill press, preferably with a lip-and-spur bit, drill

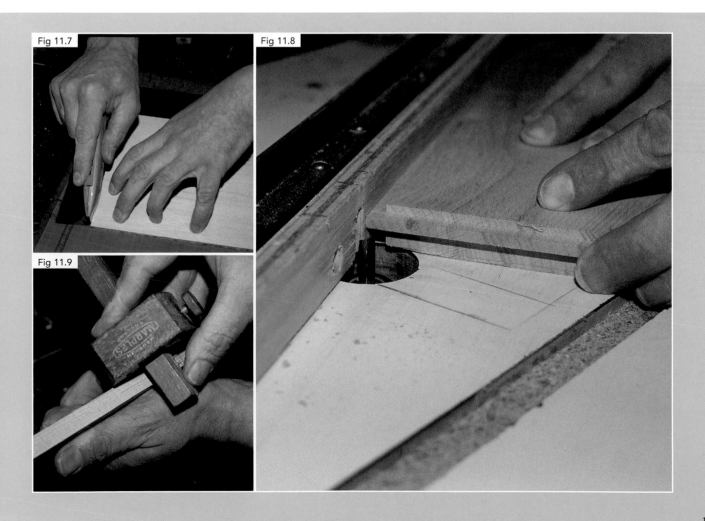

Fig 11.7

Fig 11.8

Fig 11.9

slowly and carefully through to the other side, clearing the shavings regularly. If the gods are smiling, the hole which emerges on the other side will be centered exactly on the gauged line. However, it is possible that the drill will have wandered. Drill bits do have a tendency to find the path of least resistance. Harder wood and the direction of the grain can make a significant contribution to where the drill emerges. There are several ways of dealing with this problem. One is to drill the hole and then plane the wood so that the wood finishes parallel with the hole. Another, which I prefer, is to tilt the machine vise slightly so that it holds the hinge at the correct angle and the hole emerges in the center.

If the first hole emerged dead center, drill the second about 30mm (1¼in) from the first. If either of the holes need to be re-drilled, work outward towards the ends of the hinge pieces. It can sometimes take several attempts before a hole comes out in exactly the right position.

Once you are satisfied with the two holes, mark the hinges in some way to avoid mixing them up, then saw them off 7mm (⁹⁄₃₂in) from the center of the hole. Finally, on the sanding disc or shooting board, make sure that these four ends are parallel to the hole and finish 6.5mm (¼in) from the center. I use a little jig, which uses a piece of brass rod through the pivot holes, for this. (See Fig 9.24, p 99.) Sand the end of the hinge until the rod is stopped, by the jig, from going any further.

It is now time to cut the knuckles of the hinge. Once again there is no right and wrong way of doing this. With careful marking out there's no reason why a backsaw to make the vertical cut, a coping saw to remove the waste, and a chisel for squaring off can't be used. You could even use a table saw by passing the hinge vertically across the blade. My method uses an inverted router.

Bolt a wooden fence onto the miter fence and C-clamp one of the shorter hinge pieces with a piece of waste wood behind it: this will prevent any tear-out at the back of the cut. Using a long-reach, 5mm (¹³⁄₆₄in), straight router cutter, rout a slot in the hinge about 3mm (³⁄₃₂in) in from the edge. Repeat this for the other short piece. For the two longer pieces, rout the slot 8mm (⁵⁄₁₆in) in from the same edge, with the hinge C-clamped to the fence once again. To rout the rest of the slots that form the knuckle of the hinge on each piece, position this first slot with a pin in the fence.

With all the slots cut, saw off the waste pins on either side and check that the pieces fit together. They should fit snugly and not need any force. If they do need slight adjustments, ease them very carefully with a chisel or sand them very lightly. To do this, plane a piece of waste wood to an exact fit between the prongs and wrap abrasive paper around it. Keep the abrasive tight on the block and take care not to round the corners of the pins. My rule of thumb for the fit of the knuckles is that

Fig 11.10 *The hinge held in the machine vise on the drill press*

Fig 11.11 *It took me two attempts before these holes emerged in the correct place*

Fig 11.12 *Hinge pieces marked and ready to separate*

Fig 11.13 *Sanding the ends of the hinges parallel to the hole*

Fig 11.14 *Even using the router, I like to roughly mark the position of the slots*

Fig 11.15 *Cutting the first slot*

Fig 11.16 *Positioning the first slot on the pin*

Fig 11.17 *The waste 'half pin' must be sawn off*

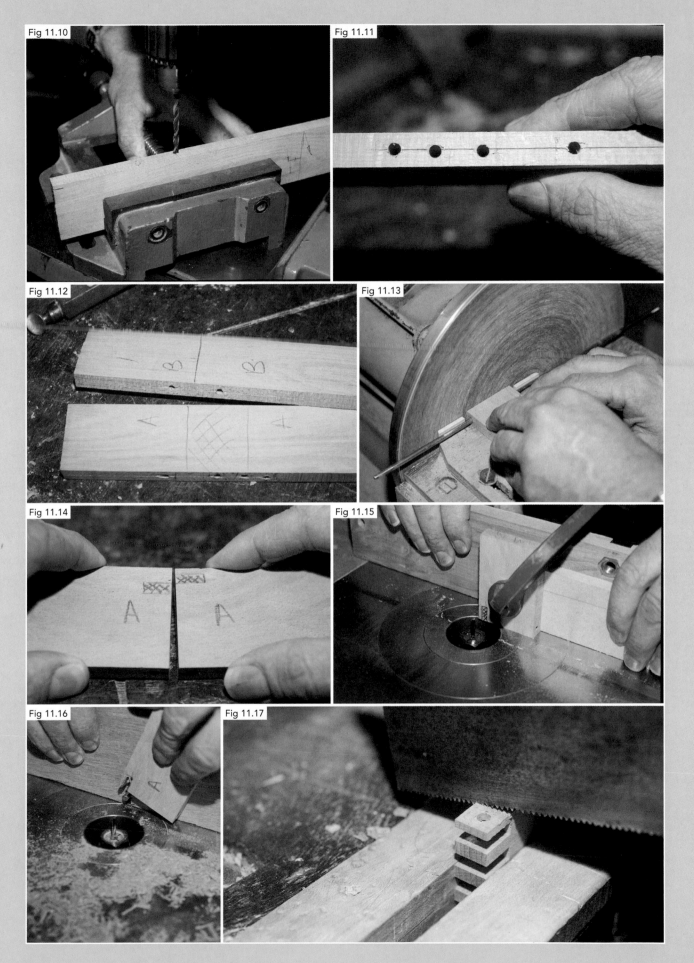

Fig 11.10

Fig 11.11

Fig 11.12

Fig 11.13

Fig 11.14

Fig 11.15

Fig 11.16

Fig 11.17

if either side of the hinge does not fall under its own weight when the pivot is in place, it needs a little more easing.

Using the hole as the center, plane and sand a semicircle onto the edge of each hinge piece. I am stressing that the hole is the center because it may be that the hole does not run parallel to the edges of the hinge. Sand the knuckles to 240 grit then insert the dowel pivots. There are two dowel pivots on each hinge, inserted one from either side, leaving a gap of about 0.5mm ($^1/_{64}$in) in the center of each. Glue them in place with a drop of superglue. Saw off the excess pivot, leaving it slightly proud, then sand the ends flat.

Fitting the hinges to the box

Back to the box. Place the hinges on the back of the box and pencil two lines square across it, either side of the hinge. These lines don't need to be spot-on accurate. They're really more of a guide to show you when to start checking. At this point make sure that both ends of the box are absolutely square to the bottom. If the hinges aren't parallel, they won't work very well.

With a straight cutter in the router (I used an 18mm ($^3/_4$in) cutter but the size isn't that critical) and the fence set so that a trench is cut 2–3mm (approx. $^1/_8$in) inside the lines, rout a trench to a depth which leaves 10mm ($^{13}/_{32}$in) of wood on the box. Reset the cutter for a trench 9mm ($^3/_8$in) in and take a few final slivers off either side, offering the hinge into the trench each time until it's a snug fit.

If your hinges are absolutely identical in width then the trenches can be cut working from either end of the box. In this case the final cut will be the last for both hinges. Mine are seldom that accurate so right at the end I always treat each hinge as an individual.

The holes for the screws can now be marked and drilled. Drill straight 8mm ($^5/_{16}$in) holes, then use a lip-and-spur bit, which will leave a clear center 'V' at the bottom of the hole.

Cutting off the lid

Now cut the box in two. As with skinning cats, there is more than one way to do this. It can be done by hand, marking a pencil line all the way around and cutting with a backsaw. Using a band saw with a good sharp blade is another possibility and is a method I have used, but I've always been anxious about the cut being on the underside of the box where I can't see it. I have also used an electric jigsaw for this job. With a jigsaw, starting the cut is not easy, but it does produce a good finish and it is possible, by inserting wedges of wood in the kerf, to work your way around the box with the box held in the vise. The last time I had to do this job I used my new table saw and there's no doubt in my mind that this is the best way. Whichever method you use, with the box cut into two, the lid and base will almost certainly need planing, if only to remove saw marks. Be very careful with this. Keep it

Fig 11.18 *Using the sanding disc for rounding off the knuckles*

Fig 11.19 *A drop of superglue secures the pivot*

Fig 11.20 *Marking the position of the hinges on the back of the box*

Fig 11.21 *Offering up the hinge to its trench*

Fig 11.22 *One last pass across the router takes the trench down to size*

Fig 11.23 *Drilling the 8mm ($^5/_{16}$in) holes in the back of the hinges*

Fig 11.24 *Separating the box from the lid using a jigsaw*

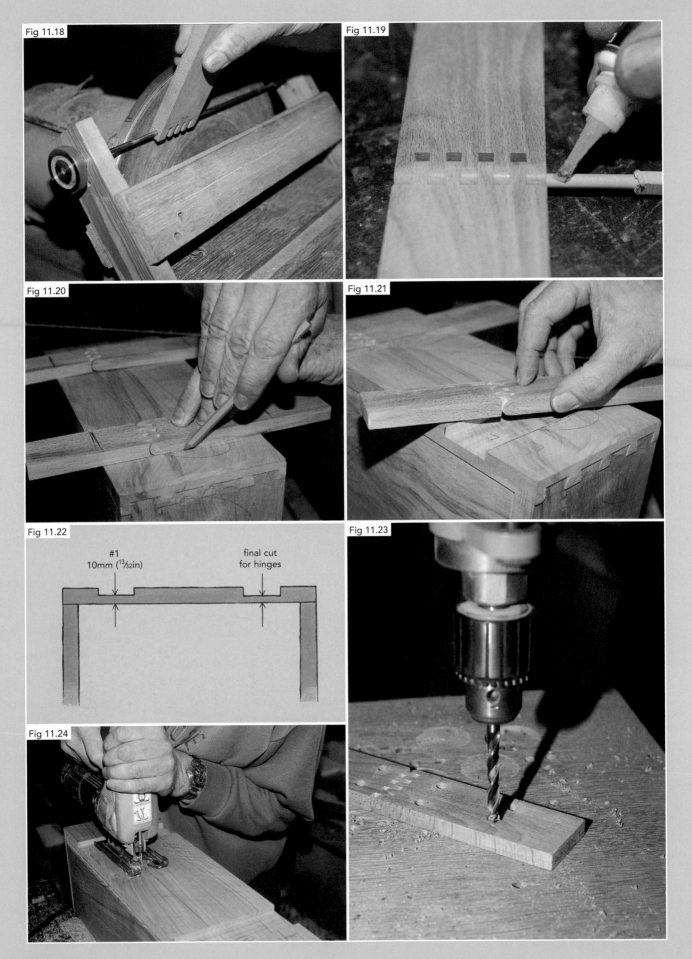

Fig 11.18

Fig 11.19

Fig 11.20

Fig 11.21

Fig 11.22

#1
10mm (¹³⁄₃₂in)

final cut
for hinges

Fig 11.23

Fig 11.24

129

to an absolute minimum as it's all too easy to chase round and round the edge in the quest for a perfect fit and end up with far too small a pin on the corners. Sand these corners to 240 grit.

Hold the box in the vise with four spacers of folded paper along the back edge. The thickness of four pieces of copier paper will give a clearance of about 0.4mm ($^1/_{64}$in). With the hinge in position, drill through two of the holes (one at the top and one at the bottom) with a 1.5mm bit, to a depth of 5mm ($^{13}/_{64}$in). Use a piece of dowel as a depth stop. Remove the hinge and enlarge the 1.5mm ($^1/_{16}$in) hole to 3.5mm ($^9/_{64}$in). Using two pairs of $^5/_8$in, No. 4 round-head screws, fix the hinges in position. Using only two screws at this stage gives you much more chance to right any wrongs.

Take a deep breath and open the lid. With any luck, it should open smoothly. If it doesn't, the chances are that something is inaccurate and you might have to go back to the hinge stage and possibly even start the hinges again. If all is well, the lid can be removed and the outside of the lid and box planed to their final thickness, which in this case was 16mm ($^5/_8$in).

Sand the box and lid to 120 grit and continue sanding to 400 grit, on the back only. With this finished, remove the sharp corners at the back of the lid and box and re-fit the hinge, this time using all the screw holes.

The disc

Unfortunately, it's now time to tackle the disc. I say unfortunately because, having almost finished a gorgeous-looking box, I am now suggesting that you clamp it into the vise and take a router to it. It's a case of omelettes and eggs I'm afraid, so grit your teeth, check that there are no lumps of old glue stuck to the vise jaws (it might be a good idea to use clean plywood or supplementary hardwood cheeks to protect the box) and clamp it into the vise.

With a soft pencil, mark a rough circle where you want the disc to be. Mine looked best just under one-third of the way from the left-hand side – 97mm (3$^3/_4$in) from one end and 221mm (8$^3/_4$in) from the other. Drill a 5mm ($^{13}/_{64}$in) hole to a depth of 7mm ($^9/_{32}$in) to take the pin on the circle-cutting jig. (See jigs in Chapter 2, p 16.) Set up the router with the circle-cutting plate and set the depth of cut to 5mm ($^{13}/_{64}$in) on the depth stop. Locate the pin in the center hole, then start up the router. Plunge in the cutter and rout out a circular channel. If something goes wrong and the outside of the channel is not a perfect circle, there's no harm in increasing the size of this circle slightly. Certainly the first time I tried this on a near-finished box I did it in two stages.

Once you are satisfied with the channel, remove the pin from the jig and rout out the rest of the waste freehand. Finish by scraping with the back of a broad chisel.

Fig 11.25 *With the 8mm ($^5/_{16}$in) hole drilled, the 1.5mm ($^1/_{16}$in) hole is next and, finally, the hole on the underside of the hinge is enlarged to 3.5mm ($^9/_{64}$in)*

Fig 11.26 *A dowel depth stop is a good idea*

Fig 11.27 *A circle-cutting jig*

Fig 11.28 *A circular trench is cut*

Fig 11.29 *Using a large chisel to scrape the bottom clean*

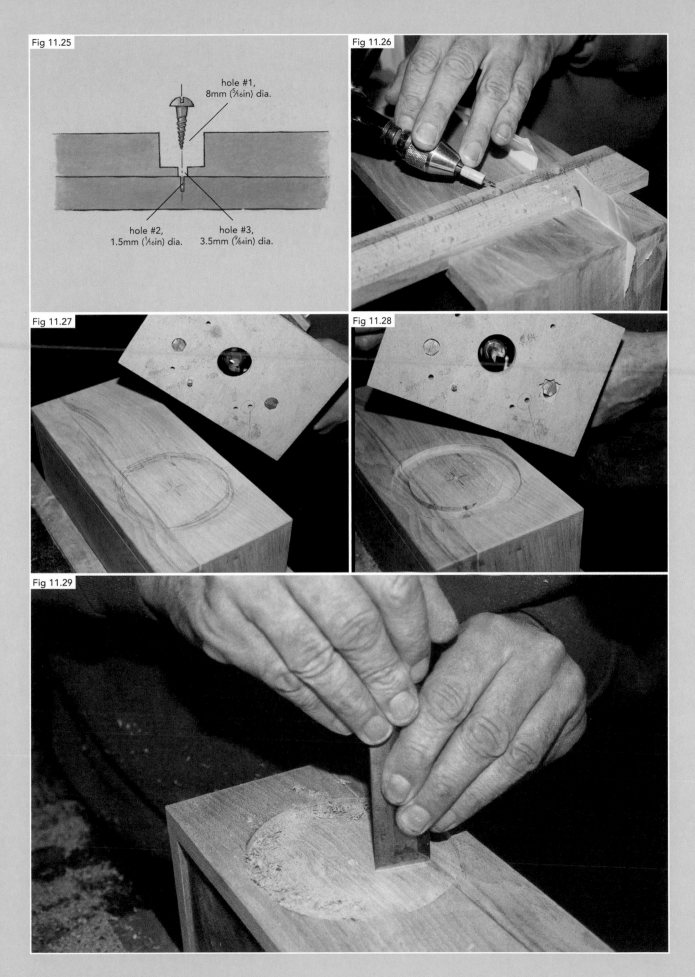

Fig 11.25

hole #1,
8mm (⁵⁄₁₆in) dia.

hole #2,
1.5mm (¹⁄₁₆in) dia.

hole #3,
3.5mm (⁹⁄₆₄in) dia.

Fig 11.26

Fig 11.27

Fig 11.28

Fig 11.29

You now need to cut a disc of wood at least 15mm ($^{19}/_{32}$in) thick. I suggest you do this by marking out a circle using a pair of compasses or dividers, then cutting the circle to just outside this line, as neatly as possible, using a band saw or coping saw. Drill a hole, about 15mm $^{19}/_{32}$in) deep, in the center of this circle and use a circle-sanding jig – a fancy name for a batten pivoted on the sanding disc table with a bolt sticking up (see jigs in Chapter 2, p 16) – to sand the outside edge to a perfect circle. The disc must be 1.5–2mm (approx. $^{1}/_{16}$in) smaller in diameter than the cut-out. Center it using some of the plastic draft excluder. My excluder is 0.6mm ($^{3}/_{64}$in) thick; if I want a size that is in between one and two thicknesses, I stick some masking tape to it.

With the disc in position, mark the line of the lid and cut the top segment off by sawing on the downside of the line. Reduce the thickness of the bottom piece to 15mm ($^{19}/_{32}$in) – this will remove the center hole. A band saw is a natural choice for this job but a backsaw will work equally well.

Flatten the back of the bottom piece, using a plane or abrasive, then saw off the flat (chord is the correct mathematical term) so that it sits about 13mm ($^{1}/_{2}$in) below the level of the lid. Sand this chord square and smooth and then, using the plastic spacer, glue the bottom piece of the circle into place. When the glue has hardened, plane and sand the front of the box.

You can now glue the top piece of the circle, which remained at 15mm ($^{19}/_{32}$in), in position using the same spacers. If it overhangs the lid slightly, plane it flush once the glue has hardened.

Shaping the handle

Finally, the handle can be shaped. You can use a sharp chisel, paring upwards, a rasp, or even the edge of a rotating sanding disc. Whatever you choose though, it's best to finish off by using a shaped, cork block and sandpaper.

Finishing the hinges

Once you've finished the handle, it's back to the hinges. Plane these to a slight taper from the knuckle outwards and then, using the same wood as the disc – bog oak in my case – cut a length of 8mm ($^{5}/_{16}$in) dowel, about 300mm (12in), into 7mm ($^{9}/_{32}$in) pegs. Drop a little glue on the inside of the hinge hole and tap these pegs home. Once the glue has set, trim the pegs so that they are all the same length. Do this by carefully cutting them towards the center with a very sharp chisel or, taking great care, using the edge of a sanding disc.

Fig 11.30 *A rough circle cut out from a piece of bog oak*

Fig 11.31 *A circle-sanding jig*

Fig 11.32 *A piece of plastic draft excluder keeps the gap even*

Fig 11.33 *The bog oak disc is sawn in two*

Fig 11.34 *Gluing the disc in place*

Fig 11.35 *Planing the disc flush with the front of the box*

Fig 11.36 *Shaping the handle*

Fig 11.37 *Bog oak pegs are used to cover the screws*

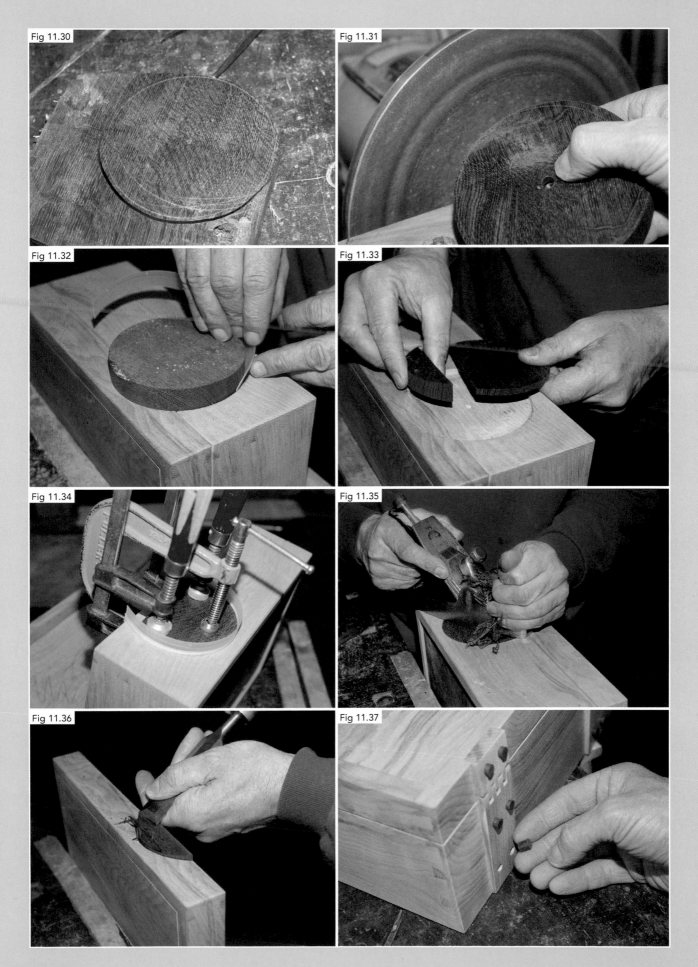

Fig 11.30

Fig 11.31

Fig 11.32

Fig 11.33

Fig 11.34

Fig 11.35

Fig 11.36

Fig 11.37

CHESS
BOX

A chess box is one of those boxes that definitely has to be worked from the inside out, so strictly speaking, this box should be in the 'From the Inside Out' section. However, as it has a back hinge and is similar in a lot of ways to the jewelry box, I think it is best here.

The place to start is with the chesspieces. I know there are people who collect chess sets and I know there are many wonderful and bizarre sets out there, but I wanted a set that would be used. I very quickly learned that no serious chess player would play with anything other than a Staunton set. It seemed that weight, too, was important. Triple-weighted was the best and a 95mm (3¾in) king was the correct tournament height. It certainly wasn't a cheap set to buy but I wanted to make a very special box, so the pieces had to be right.

Having determined the style and size of the chess set to be stored, I turned my attention to the board. It seems that 55mm (2¼in) squares are the ideal size for these pieces, though 50mm (2in) would do at a pinch.

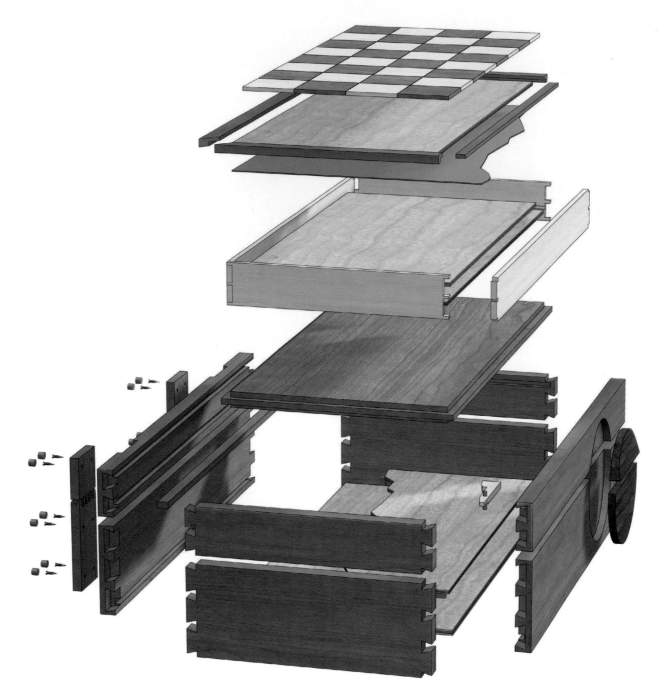

THE WOOD

In this case I have used American black walnut. I wanted something sumptuous and rich that would contrast well with the sycamore. It also had to be fairly formal and conservative, nothing too wild or flamboyant. As for the beech jewelry box (see Chapter 11, p 121) I used a bog oak disc to add some interest to an otherwise fairly plain front.

THE PROCESS

Calculating the box size

If the set you're using is exactly the same size as mine, simply read off my dimensions. Otherwise work from the pieces outwards as follows.

Measure the diameter of the base for each of the principal pieces, allow an extra 6mm (1/4in) for the leather, and 8mm (5/16in) between each piece. Allow 15mm (19/32in) above the king (the largest piece), 25mm (1in) to separate the pieces in the top row from the pawns which are laid out in the bottom row, and a further 15mm (19/32in) below the pawns. These calculations will give the minimum internal dimensions for the tray, which in my case was 430 × 200mm (17 × 8in).

The board is simpler to work out. The size of each square is dictated by the diameter of the base of the king. The base of my king was 42mm (1⁵/₈in) and I had decided on a square of 55mm (2³/₁₆in). With 64 squares on a chessboard this made the size of half a board 476 × 238mm (16¹⁵/₁₆ × 9³/₈in), including an 18mm (³/₄in) border. As these dimensions are larger than the tray size, they are the ones that dictate the length and breadth of the box.

The height required is arrived at through the following series of calculations which start, believe it or not, with the thickness of the lid. I strongly recommend drawing this out full size.

- Start with the thickness of the lid – for my box this was 15mm (19/32in)
- Add the thickness of the board – 20mm (³/₄in)
- Add the diameter of the king plus 6mm (1/4in) – 48mm (1⁷/₈in)
- Add the thickness of the tray bottom – 4mm (⁵/₃₂in)
- Add the well on the underside of the tray – 5mm (¹³/₆₄in)
- Draw in the board locator (strip of wood at the back of the lid behind which the board sits) underneath the board – 5mm (¹³/₆₄in)
- Measure up from the base of the tray to 2mm (⁵/₆₄in) below the board locator: this will give the position of the top tray
- From the tray base add the diameter of the king plus 6mm (1/4in) – 48mm (1⁷/₈in)
- Add the box base – 4mm (⁵/₃₂in)
- Add the well on the bottom of the box – 8mm (⁵/₁₆in)
- Finally, calculate the lid line so it overlaps the tray by 10mm (³/₈in)

According to these calculations, the minimum height required is 147mm (5²³/₃₂in), split 52/95mm (2/3²³/₃₂in) between the lid and the box. When I looked at the full-size plan for my box, drawn following these sizes, I decided that the lid line was a little bit low so I increased the depth of the bottom layer by 5mm (¹³/₆₄in). This made the final dimensions 152mm (5¹⁵/₁₆in) with a 52/100mm (2/3¹⁵/₁₆in) split.

Don't get too hung up on these figures. They more or less shredded my brain. Just put some chesspieces and some examples of wood onto a piece of paper on the bench, and all will become clear. It's a moot point whether the box or the board should be made first. I chose the box. Follow the same method as for the jewelry box (see Chapter 11, p 121). However, before you glue up, you must do two more things: cut the grooves for the catch and rout the groove for the board locator.

The catch

Once you have cut the box open and planed and sanded the edges, you can drill the lid for the pivot and make the catch. I put a lot of thinking time into this catch. My first idea, for a simple turnbuckle, failed totally. The catch I finally devised seems to combine the qualities of being unobtrusive, compact and easy to use and, its spring mechanism – gravity – will never fail. Rather than giving a convoluted explanation of how to make this catch, I have given a clear series of diagrams (see Fig 12.1).

The board

With your catch made, put the box to one side and start work on the board. This is made in two halves. For the first half, cut six pieces of 1.5mm ($\frac{1}{16}$in) plywood, all 255 × 510mm (10 × 20in).

If you have a veneer press, the next job is fairly straightforward. If you don't, prepare two pieces of thick MDF or chipboard, 25mm (1in) or more, by cutting them roughly to size – just over 255 × 510mm (10 × 20in) – and, if you work like me, have just about every clamp in the workshop standing by.

Using a reasonably sized paintbrush – 25–38mm (1–1$\frac{1}{2}$in) – quickly cover one piece of the plywood with slightly diluted PVA. Pop another piece on top, cover it with PVA, then complete the sandwich with a third piece. Now clamp the whole thing up tight. This method of making plywood results in a very stable piece of 5mm ($\frac{13}{64}$in) plywood. (I know 3 × 1.5 = 4.5 but somehow, when you glue three pieces of 1.5mm plywood together it comes to 5.)

The squares

Now for the squares. For these I used 5mm ($\frac{13}{64}$in) American black walnut and sycamore. The first job is to cut the wood for the squares into strips 55mm (2$\frac{1}{4}$in) wide. If you have a good table saw this will not present much of a problem. If a band saw or radial arm saw is all you have to rip with, do not despair. In fact, don't even despair if you have no powered saw at all. Just cut the strips as close to 55mm (2$\frac{1}{4}$in) as you can, then crosscut them as close to 55mm (2$\frac{1}{4}$in), as accurately as possible.

A powered saw may not be necessary but a sanding disc, I think, is, especially if you don't have an accurate table saw. Starting with the long grain, and using a 'T' jig (see Chapter 2, p 18), sand all the pieces on one edge. Next, without using the jig, sand an end-grain edge square to the finished long-grain edge. The remaining two edges can then be sanded using the 'T' jig once again.

If you have worked logically and carefully, you should now have two neat piles of 35 precisely dimensioned squares, one black pile and one white. I cut 35 because it's not a bad idea to make three extra of each color to cover all eventualities.

Fig 12.1 *The gravity catch*

Fig 12.2 *Checking that the hinges fit*

Fig 12.3 *Gluing and clamping up a plywood sandwich*

Fig 12.4 *Using the 'T' jig*

Fig 12.5 *Making sure the battens are exactly square*

These squares now need to be glued to the plywood. Clamp two battens (waste wood planed with one straight edge) to the plywood, leaving a generous border all round. Make sure they are square to one another. For the spacers I used some old plastic draft excluder which I found knocking around in the workshop. Plastic margarine containers would work just as well; detergent bottles might be a bit curvy and possibly inclined to spring things out of place. Anything that has a consistent thickness and that is totally impervious to the stickiness of PVA can be used.

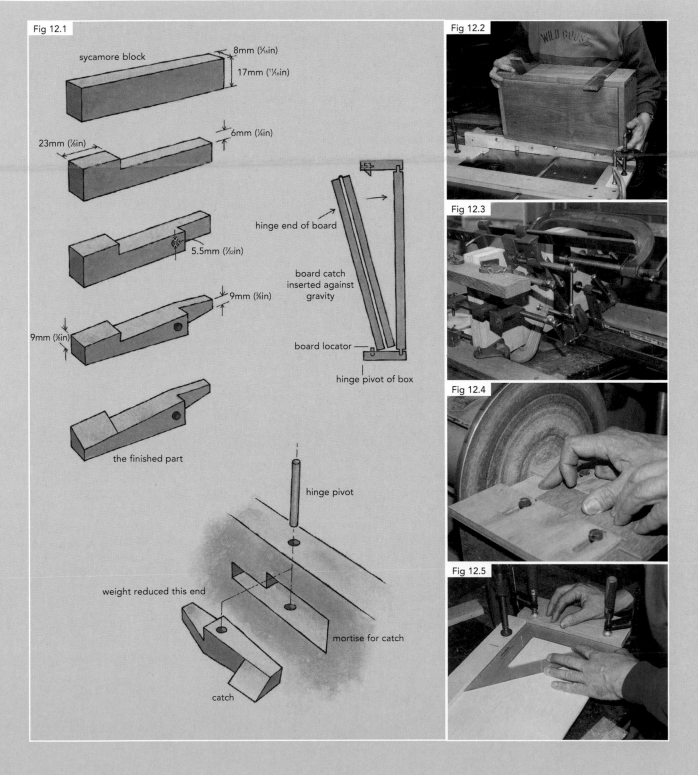

Fig 12.1

sycamore block

8mm (⁵⁄₁₆in)

17mm (¹¹⁄₁₆in)

6mm (¼in)

23mm (⅞in)

5.5mm (⁷⁄₃₂in)

hinge end of board

board catch inserted against gravity

9mm (⅜in)

9mm (⅜in)

board locator

the finished part

hinge pivot of box

hinge pivot

weight reduced this end

mortise for catch

catch

Fig 12.2

Fig 12.3

Fig 12.4

Fig 12.5

At this point I gave some long and serious thought as to whether the grain should all run the same way or in alternate directions. I don't think there's that much in it but on balance I prefer the grain all running in one direction, and apart from the finished appearance, it definitely makes cleaning up the surface of the board much easier.

You now need to work quite quickly. Starting at the right-hand corner with a white square, place a dab of glue in the center of the square and press it into place. Do the same for each square, alternating colors and fixing spacers in between. After each row, check that the squares are aligned by using a straightedge. After the fourth row, and using two more battens, all of the squares can be pulled up hard against their spacers by using sash clamps. Do not tighten these clamps up too hard: if you do there is a serious danger of the squares curving away from the plywood and ending up in a heap in the middle of the bench!

You could leave it there but I didn't. I have a strong aversion to leaving glue to go off completely unclamped. I left the squares for around 10 minutes and then, once the glue was holding the squares but before it was dry, I pulled out all the spacers and clamped the board up between two pieces of MDF. Try as I might I couldn't think of a way of clamping the squares both together and down at the same time. I did experiment with a contact adhesive but in the end I definitely came down in favor of PVA.

Make the second half of the board in exactly the same way.

Edging the board

The next job is to prepare the wood for the edging. You need two pieces of 21 × 11 × 500mm ($^7/_8$ × $^7/_{16}$ × 20in), four pieces of 21 × 11 × 250mm ($^7/_8$ × $^7/_{16}$ × 10in) and two pieces of 5 × 12 × 500mm ($^{13}/_{64}$ × $^1/_2$ × 20in). I think these pieces look better in the principal wood of the box – in this case, walnut.

Plane the hinge edge of the plywood to fractionally short of the squares – about 0.5mm ($^1/_{64}$in) – then move to the router and rout 10mm ($^3/_8$in) of the plywood away to form a 10mm ($^3/_8$in) rabbet underneath the squares.

The next step is to glue the 5 × 12mm ($^{13}/_{64}$ × $^1/_2$in) lipping to the long center edge; the lipping will be slightly oversize at this point. I tried masking tape for this job but while it is strong enough, it couldn't hold the lipping to the underside of the squares and the edge of the plywood, so I gave up after a dummy run and used C-clamps and sash clamps instead.

Lay the edging out around the board, preferably with the grain running around the miters. For this to work all the way around the board, however, the edging would have to come from one single length, which is unlikely. Look carefully at the grain and match it as closely as possible. Number the pieces and cut a rough miter on the ends. I always find it helpful to do this. If I don't, I invariably get in a muddle and mix pieces up. Sand the underside and inside edge of each piece.

Once the glue on the lipping is dry, plane the lipping flush to the underside of the plywood. The plywood now needs to be cut to exactly 10mm (^{3}/$_8$in) from the squares. I used a simple jig for this. By clamping a piece of MDF to the fence of my table saw, slightly higher than the table, I was able to run the squares against the fence, so I didn't have to rely on pencil lines.

The next job is to cut a 9.5 × 5mm (^{3}/$_8$ × ^{13}/$_{64}$in) rabbet on the edging. For this job, it is back to the router.

Mark a pencil line 12mm (^{1}/$_2$in) in, all around the edge of the board, and plane a 12 × 0.5mm (^{1}/$_2$ × ^{1}/$_{64}$in) chamfer, 0.5mm (^{1}/$_{64}$in) being the thickness of the leather. I say plane a chamfer. It is possible to set the router up for this job, but I think, if your plane is sharp, it's probably not worth the time and hassle.

Fig 12.6 *Gluing down the squares*

Fig 12.7 *Pulling the squares up to the battens with sash clamps*

Fig 12.8 *Forming a rabbet underneath the squares*

Fig 12.9 *Plane the lipping flush with the bottom of the plywood*

Fig 12.10 *The edging is rabbeted around the rest of the board*

Fig 12.11 *Chamfering the underside of the plywood to allow the leather to finish flush with the edging*

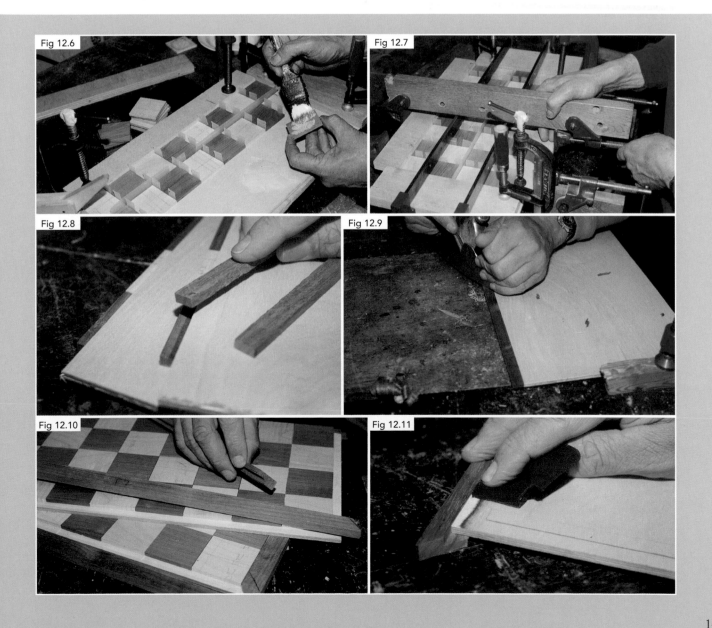

Fig 12.6

Fig 12.7

Fig 12.8

Fig 12.9

Fig 12.10

Fig 12.11

Now for the bit I really don't like. It was some time ago that I rashly agreed to whip a bit of beading around a small armchair table for someone. It was an unmitigated disaster. I kept having to plane a little bit more off the edge of the table top: it refused to become square and no matter how many times I re-cut the miters I could not get them to pull up tight. At least this job involves only three sides. Start by mitering the two short sides and one long side (the front). I use a 45° block on the sanding disc table for miters and I'm quite happy with the accuracy.

Tape the side piece in its correct position and tape the long front piece in position with its miter hard up against the side piece. Carefully mark the other end of the long piece with a very fine pencil or scriber, then sand or shoot a miter down to this line. Offer up the third piece to check it. In essence, what you've got to achieve is a gap equal to the gap around the squares.

Hinging the board

Rout a shallow rabbet for the moiré hinge, about 30mm (1¼in) wide and as deep as the moiré is thick – 0.4mm (¹⁄₆₄in). Gluing these edging pieces on is surprisingly difficult. Actually, gluing them is easy – it's clamping them that's a bit of a problem. In the end I used a band clamp, which ensured that the miters were pulled up tight, several blocks and C-clamps, which ensured that the edging was kept hard on the plywood. I've no doubt that there are many other solutions.

Plane the surface of the board with an ultra-sharp blade then sand to 400 grit. Next, plane and sand the edges of the board to get a good fit inside the lid; for this it should be about 2mm (⁵⁄₆₄in) smaller than the inside of the lid all round.

With the two halves of the board taped together and lying on a flat surface, use PVA to glue a strip of moiré into its channel. This will reinforce the leather hinge.

At this point it's a good idea to oil and wax the board. If this is done now there is no chance of the oil getting onto the leather.

Leather comes in many shapes and sizes. You can buy a whole side of a cow, a goat skin or even soft gloving leather from sheep. Or you can buy offcuts of these. They are all different thicknesses and available in many different colors. For this job I think a pig or sheep's hide is best, preferably in a dark, rich color. (Pig and sheep leather is thinner, softer and more pliable than cow.) Leather can also be bought for use suede-side or smooth-side up. For this box I chose to use a pig skin suede-side up, and I used the same leather for lining the trays and sticking to the bottom of the chesspieces. Suede has a lovely soft, sensuous feel but it very quickly picks up dust and dirt.

Spread the leather out on a cutting board; don't stretch it, just lie it flat and free of wrinkles and tape it down. Cut out a square to fit the bottom of the board exactly. Cover the board with a rubber-

Fig 12.12 *The miter on the corner of the edging*

Fig 12.13 *Securing the edging using a band clamp*

Fig 12.14 *Somewhat complicated clamping ensures that the edging is pulled up tight*

Fig 12.15 *The lipping is all trimmed to size*

Fig 12.16 *A freshly sharpened plane is a must for this job*

Fig 12.17 *A strip of moiré strengthens the hinge*

Fig 12.12

Fig 12.13

Fig 12.14

Fig 12.15

Fig 12.16

Fig 12.17

based glue, such as Copydex, which won't penetrate the leather and, working from the center out, stick the leather down, stretching or contracting it slightly as necessary to achieve a good fit against the walnut lipping. A practice run with a piece of scrap leather might well be a good idea. Line the inside of the box with moiré (see Chapter 11, p 124).

Miter four pieces of sycamore, of 49mm ($1^{15}/_{16}$in) width, around the inside of the box but don't glue these in until right at the end when you are sure that everything fits as it should.

The tray

Now we move on to the tray. I recommend using 6–6.5mm (about $^{1}/_{4}$in) sycamore for the tray sides. Dovetail and make these as described under trays in Chapter 3 (see p 28).

To mark and cut out the holes for the chesspieces, mark around one each of the six different pieces onto small bits of paper using a pencil held at 90° to the paper. This should add about 2.5mm ($^{3}/_{32}$in) all round to each shape. For the knight, cut around the pencil line. For all the other pieces, fold the paper in half before cutting around the pencil line. Unfolded you will have the whole piece symmetrically cut out. You can then measure the total space these will occupy and find the space to leave between each. Measure the base of each of the paper cut-outs and add these together, then add another rook, knight and bishop. This will give you the total space taken up by the eight pieces. Subtract this from the length of the tray to find the space that is left on the tray. For even spaces, divide this figure by nine: as there are eight pieces there will be nine spaces.

The pawns can either sit centrally beneath the principal piece above, or be spaced evenly in the tray. Mine are spaced evenly so it was simply a question of doing a similar calculation. For the row of pawns, every piece is the same size. Multiply the base of one pawn by eight, subtract this from the inside of the tray, and divide by nine to find the space.

On a larger-than-necessary piece of 4mm ($^{5}/_{32}$in) plywood, draw two base lines, one for the the king and one for a pawn, so that they are spaced reasonably apart. Draw around each of these paper shapes, leaving the correct space between them. The knights should face inwards, towards their queen. I've got a feeling that this all sounds rather more complicated than it is. Once you are doing it, it will become obvious.

Note that I have only mentioned, up to now, one of the layers of pieces. This is because the spacing is different for the top or tray layer. All right, I'll own up. It was going to be the same until I discovered that, with only 8mm ($^{5}/_{16}$in) or so of sycamore protruding above the side of the box, it was virtually impossible to grip and take out the tray, even when it wasn't fully laden with 16 triple-weighted

Fig 12.18 *These pieces of sycamore support the top tray*

Fig 12.19 *Cutting the paper with a fold in the center ensures that the template is symmetrical*

Fig 12.20 *Marking the position for the holes on the plywood*

Fig 12.21 *The base line for every piece is cut first*

Fig 12.22 *Cutting the base line using the fence on the router*

Fig 12.23 *'Freehanding' the holes*

chesspieces. My solution to this little conundrum was to pack the pieces slightly closer together in the tray and leave a space either end (for a pen?) so that the tray can be gripped positively from the inside.

With the two pieces of plywood marked out, pop a straight, single-fluted cutter – about 4mm ($^5/_{32}$in) – into the router, set the fence so that the cutter will emerge just within the hole, barely touching the base line, and rout the base line of each piece. Now, do away with the fence and work freehand. Drawing the plywood towards you, cut out the space for each piece. I experimented with a two-flute cutter but found that a single-flute, high-speed-steel (HSS) cutter worked best – possibly because it was sharper. I strongly suggest that you cut out a couple of holes on a piece of waste plywood first and, using an offcut of the leather, check that the chesspiece nestles comfortably in its space. It shouldn't fall too far through or it will be difficult to take out but on the other hand, it shouldn't sit too proud or the lid will touch it when it shuts.

Cut the plywood to size, leaving a gap for the leather of about 2mm ($^5/_{64}$in) all around.

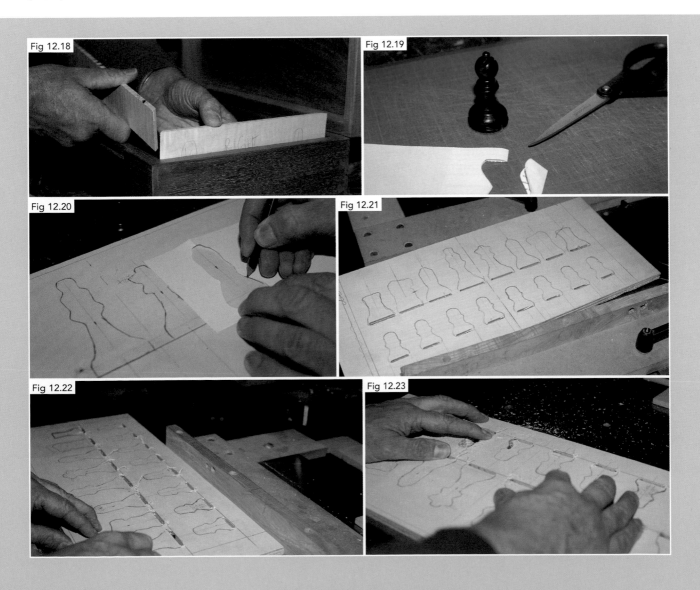

Fig 12.18

Fig 12.19

Fig 12.20

Fig 12.21

Fig 12.22

Fig 12.23

The ribs

The ribs can now be cut and glued to the underside of the plywood. These ribs not only act as supports for the plywood, they provide strength where the plywood is weakest – between the pieces. I made my ribs from offcuts of 5mm ($^{13}/_{64}$in) sycamore but just about any material of around that thickness would do. With a bead of glue on each rib, place them in position and clamp them all down, sandwiched between two pieces of MDF, with C-clamps. It doesn't matter exactly where the ribs go as long as they support the weak places but for the top layer there must be two end ribs set 10mm ($^3/_8$in) in from the end of the plywood and finishing about 2mm ($^5/_{64}$in) shorter either end. These end ribs are 18mm ($^{23}/_{32}$in) wide; all the others are 20mm ($^{51}/_{64}$in).

Cover the bottom layer with leather first. This is the easier of the two as all the folded bits will be concealed beneath the level of the plywood. With a clean sheet of newspaper underneath, spray the plywood with the sort of adhesive used for mounting photos onto card, for example, Spray Mount. When this is done, get rid of the newspaper – the adhesive gets everywhere. Cut a piece of leather to approximately 600 × 300mm (24 × 12in) and lay it gently onto the plywood. Starting with the king and the pawn in the row beneath it, press the pieces into the leather, evening out the folds and rucks as they occur. The adhesive should stop one piece popping out as you push its neighbor in.

Once all the pieces are pushed home and you are happy with their depth, take them out, turn the plywood over and fold the leather underneath it, using a rubber-based glue to hold it down, and trim.

For the top layer, push in the pieces as before, glue the leather underneath the plywood and onto the end rib, then take it underneath the rib and glue it to the inside. The corners can be a little tricky, but it's the sort of job where, if you're good at making beds with hospital corners or brilliant at wrapping Christmas presents, you'll have no problem. Cover two pieces of card with leather to fix at either end of the tray.

Once all the leather has been tucked away out of sight, the insides can be pushed into place. Try them with all the pieces in position and check that everything fits and closes as it should. The tolerances are not huge so things may have to be adjusted slightly – now is the time to do it, not once everything has been glued into place.

When you are satisfied that everything is as it should be, oil and wax the whole thing, then glue in the leather insides. Use clamps for this, particularly for the tray as the 'handles' will put the glue joint under a fair amount of strain. The bases of my chesspieces were covered with a bright green felt. I cut this off and replaced it with leather.

I think this project is one of the most difficult in the book. It took me quite a long time to make and I was very much feeling my way along, solving the problems as I met them. I hope I've solved most of them and have been able to tell you about them before you got there. Now, all that remains to say is – good luck with your chess!

Fig 12.24 *Gluing on the ribs*

Fig 12.25 *With all the ribs in position, clamp them down*

Fig 12.26 *The end rib for the top tray is not as wide as the others – this leaves room to tuck the leather underneath*

Fig 12.27 *Working from the center outwards, push each of the pieces into the leather*

Fig 12.28 *Fold the leather under the plywood and glue it down*

Fig 12.29 *Applying rubber-based adhesive to the end rib*

Fig 12.30 *Hospital corners*

Fig 12.31 *Trimming off excess leather*

Fig 12.32 *Covering pieces of card with leather*

Fig 12.33 *Removing the original thick green felt from the bottom of the pieces*

Fig 12.34 *Gluing on leather to replace the felt*

Fig 12.35 *Let the adhesive dry on both surfaces and it works like a contact adhesive*

Fig 12.24

Fig 12.25

Fig 12.26

Fig 12.27

Fig 12.28

Fig 12.29

Fig 12.30

Fig 12.31

Fig 12.32

Fig 12.33

Fig 12.34

Fig 12.35

FROM THE INSIDE OUT

There are some boxes that just have to be approached from the inside out, usually because of what they contain. Such boxes are designed around their contents. I have to confess, I'd much rather make a box that isn't size-specific: then there is room for mistakes. Still vivid in my memory is the day I finished a gorgeous walnut stationery box. The box had been commissioned for an anniversary and time was running tight. I rubbed the last of the wax into the lusterous surface, and the box was perfect. Then, just as a final thought, I threw in a piece of A4 paper (297 × 210mm/ 11³⁄₄ × 8¹⁄₄in). It didn't fit! Somehow, somewhere, I'd got my measurements wrong. That horrible sinking feeling lives with me still. Now, when I'm doing inside-outs, I always try to have the contents themselves on the bench when I'm marking out, even if it's only a piece of paper.

Spoon box

p 151

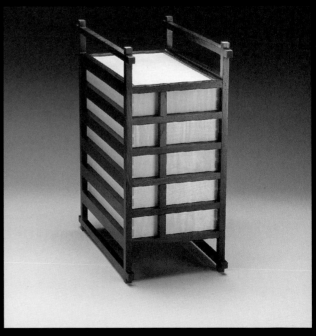

Skeleton box

p 157

inside and work outwards.

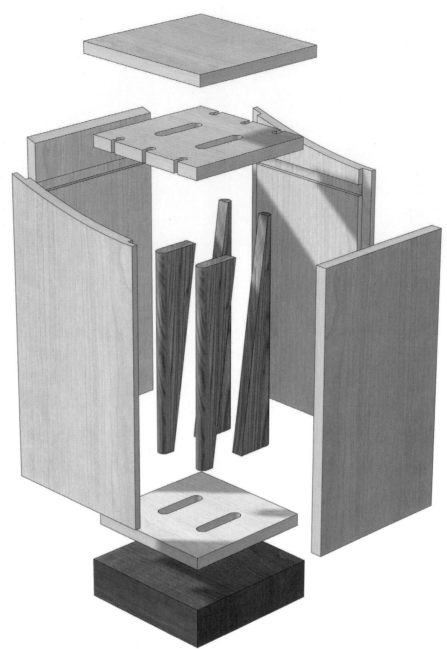

THE WOOD

For the tube part of this box, I had to start with wood that was just over twice the finished thickness; 25mm (1in) was the absolute minimum. I also wanted to use two woods that were mildly contrasting. I chose sycamore for the tube, as I had some in the required thickness and its figure varied across the width, and elm because it picked up some of the coloring in the sycamore and provided a gentle contrast.

Sycamore is normally straight grained, but European sycamore occasionally has a wavy grain, giving a figure which is much sought after. This rippled or 'fiddleback' sycamore is the traditional wood for violins, often coming from carefully tended trees, of between 50 and 100 years old, in central Europe.

THE PROCESS

Lay two spoons side by side, leaving about 2 or 3mm ($\frac{1}{16}$ or $\frac{1}{8}$in) between them, and measure the distance between their centers. A dozen spoons will need to be hung on all four sides of a block; six should fit comfortably on just two sides. So, working outwards, if one side is to take three spoons with a 25mm (1in) gap between their centers, a block 90mm ($3\frac{1}{2}$in) wide is about right (see Fig 13.2). The length of the spoons – in my case 152mm (6in) – dictates the rest of the cutting list. The measurements I've given are for my spoons. As all spoons are different, it's well worth making a test 'hanging square' first.

For the 'tube' of this box, I was very keen on the grain appearing to continue all the way around. This isn't essential and certainly isn't necessary if the grain and figure of the wood is fairly even. However, as usual, I was determined to make life as difficult as possible so I started with a piece of sycamore about 100mm (4in) greater than the length of the spoons, just over twice the width of the block and a good 5mm ($\frac{1}{4}$in) more than twice the thickness of the tube. I then marked this piece so that I could identify all the pieces and put them back together easily, and cut them out on the band saw.

Spoons all have differently shaped handles so you may have to adjust the following method and dimensions slightly.

Fig 13.1 *The various pieces machined and ready to go*

Fig 13.2 *Measuring the distance between the centers of the spoons*

Fig 13.3 *Marking the piece of wood to identify the tube sides*

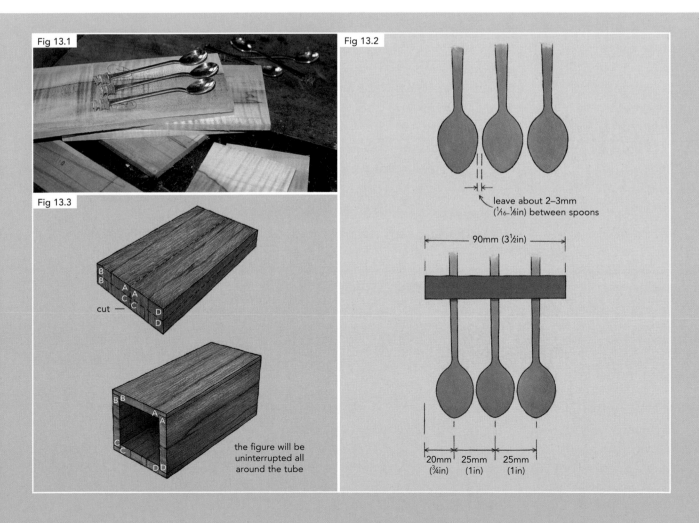

Fig 13.1

Fig 13.3

cut —

the figure will be uninterrupted all around the tube

Fig 13.2

leave about 2–3mm ($\frac{1}{16}$–$\frac{1}{8}$in) between spoons

90mm ($3\frac{1}{2}$in)

20mm ($\frac{3}{4}$in)   25mm (1in)   25mm (1in)

The spoon hanger

The first step is to mark out the top square. Mark a pencil line 8mm (⁵⁄₁₆in) in from the edge of the square. Make a cut with a backsaw or band saw as far as this line. This is so that the router cutter doesn't have to strain too hard. Set up the router with a 3mm (¹⁄₈in) straight cutter and position the fence and stops for the center cut. With this done, reposition the fence and cut the four remaining slots. Set a fence on the drill press and drill a 5.5mm (⁷⁄₃₂in) hole at the end of each slot.

For the spoon-hanging block and the bottom square, it's back to the router table. Set the fence for the central slots and work from both sides, using an 8mm (⁵⁄₁₆in) straight cutter. You either have to lower the square carefully onto the cutter or, and this is the method I prefer, plunge the cutter up towards the square.

The wedges

For the wedges, plane an 8mm (⁵⁄₁₆in) radius on two edges of the 40 × 8mm (1⁵⁄₈ × ⁵⁄₁₆in) strips and sand both faces and edges. Next, using a band saw or a backsaw, cut each strip into two wedges. Hold these four pieces in the vise, plane them all and sand off the sharp corners. You should now be able to assemble the inside to see how it looks.

The tube

Turn your attention to the tube. Assuming that the internal squares remained at 90mm (3¹⁄₂in) – it doesn't matter if they lost a fraction, just reduce the tube size accordingly – set the fence and, using a 9mm (³⁄₈in) or larger straight cutter, cut a 9mm (³⁄₈in) rabbet on the two wider tube pieces. Now switch to an 8mm (⁵⁄₁₆in) cutter and cut a trench across each of the four tube pieces.

Clean up all the inside faces of the tube and both faces of the tube top. Mask off the edge of the tube top so that it doesn't get oil on it (later, it will be glued to the tube), then oil and wax all of these surfaces. The tube can now be glued up. Check the fit of the tube over the spoon block and bottom square and sand the edges of both.

Gluing up

With this done, the inside can be glued up. Considering that one of the reasons for incorporating wedges into this design was to make the gluing up easier, this job is, unfortunately, a bit fiddly.

It's best to clamp the spoon block to the bottom square with a spacer in between. The trick then is to place a tiny blob of glue on the inside of the mortise and slide one wedge into position without it touching the glue, before sliding it sideways. You can then insert the other piece, running a dribble of glue along the center of the flat edge and placing a drop at the end of the mortise. Next, trim the ends of the wedge pieces flush below the bottom square. Sand all the surfaces of the base and glue the bottom square to it.

Fig 13.4 *Cutting the slots for the spoons*

Fig 13.5 *Drilling the holes at the end of the slots*

Fig 13.6 *Checking the spoon hanging height*

Fig 13.7 *The tube top slots into its trench*

Fig 13.8 *The two squares are held apart with a piece of waste wood and the wedges then pushed home*

Finishing

Plane and sand the tube on all four sides, then cut it to length. I cut the top freehand on the band saw. To finish, give the whole box, apart from the inside, three coats of oil before waxing.

Fig 13.4

Fig 13.5

Fig 13.6

Fig 13.7

Fig 13.8

SKELETON BOX

Perhaps this project belongs more in a 'mistakes and how to fix them' chapter than posing as a carefully designed chest of drawers – it was certainly the result of a mistake. This came about because I was simply not thinking. My brain just wasn't properly in gear. I made five identical trays, each 35mm (1³/₈in) deep. It wasn't until they were actually lined with velvet and finished and I was putting them into the box that I realized they should have been 45mm (1³/₄in) deep. I was left with five identical trays – which suggested drawers. So the sizes I've given for this project have obviously been determined by the trays which I had made. Were I making this chest from scratch, I would follow the order in which I normally make my boxes; the box first and then take the measurements from this for the trays, or in this case, the drawers.

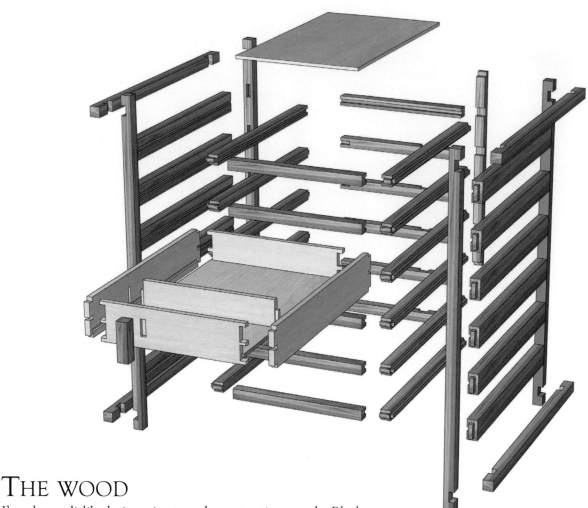

THE WOOD

I've always disliked pieces in strongly contrasting woods. Black walnut and sycamore somehow never look quite right to me. English walnut and sycamore, on the other hand, I think look a lot better. So, when I started to imagine using jet black bog oak as the frame for these drawers, the word hypocrite sprang to mind. On reflection, though, I think it's a question of proportion. Equal amounts of dark and light don't look quite right (apologies to zebras) but with the proportions in this project, I think I get away with it.

THE PROCESS

Basically, this box consists of two vertical frames, six horizontal frames and five drawers. The first job is to saw the bog oak into strips. The best way of doing this depends on what machines and tools you have available. It is a job that can be done entirely by hand, in which case I suggest you use a straight-grained and easily worked wood. At the other end of the scale, a good circular saw, a planer/thicknesser and a thicknessing drum sander would do the job with no difficulty whatsoever. Yet another course would be to ask the wood supplier to supply the material planed, thicknessed and sanded or to take it to a joiner's shop and get them to do it. With a minimum of machines though, I prefer this method.

If you have a thicknesser, thickness sufficient material, in approximate 100mm (4in) widths, to about 10.5mm ($^{21}/_{64}$in). If you don't have a thicknesser, purchase 10.5mm ($^{21}/_{64}$in) thick wood.

Sand both faces to 240 grit then plane one edge, checking that it is square, and saw off a 10.5mm ($^{21}/_{64}$in) strip. Repeat this until you have sufficient 10 × 10mm ($^3/_8$ × $^3/_8$in) sections for the job, then cut the 20 × 10mm ($^3/_4$ × $^3/_8$in) sections in the same way. The number of sections you require will depend on the size and number of drawers you want, and on the length of the pieces. For this box, I cut 34 10 × 10mm ($^3/_8$ × $^3/_8$in) sections (4 vertical frame uprights, 4 vertical frame horizontals, 12 horizontal frame sides, 12 horizontal frame fronts and backs, 1 length for handles, and 1 length for drawer stops), and 12 20 × 10mm ($^3/_4$ × $^3/_8$in) sections (all vertical frame drawer supports).

Cut every piece precisely to length. A router table is not essential for cutting the joints – each mortise could be cut by hand – but it would certainly make a vast difference both in the cutting and the marking out.

Fig 14.1 *The vertical frame*

Fig 14.2 *The horizontal frame*

Fig 14.3 *Five trays in search of a box …*

Fig 14.4 *All the pieces laid out*

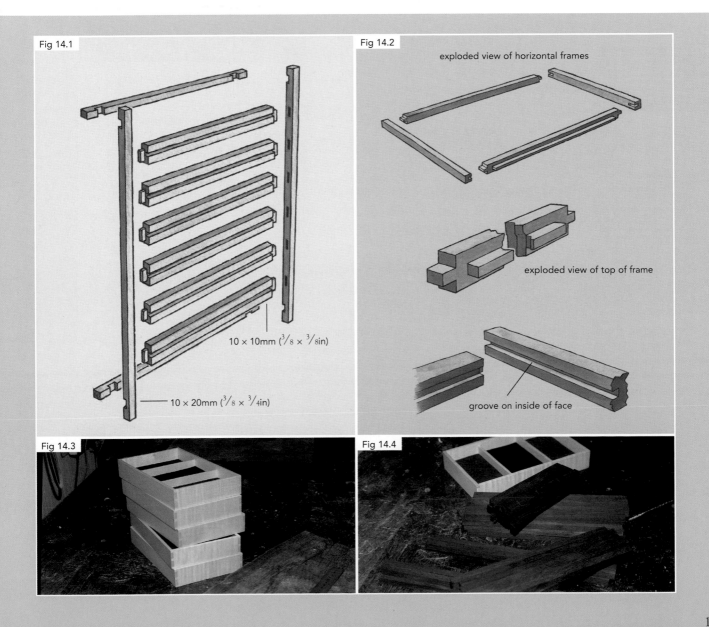

Fig 14.1

10 × 10mm ($^3/_8$ × $^3/_8$in)

10 × 20mm ($^3/_8$ × $^3/_4$in)

Fig 14.2

exploded view of horizontal frames

exploded view of top of frame

groove on inside of face

Fig 14.3

Fig 14.4

Routing the joints

For the upright, use a pair of dividers to mark the centers of each joint. With a 4mm ($^5/_{32}$in) straight cutter set to a depth of 4mm ($^5/_{32}$in), set up the router to cut a groove exactly in the center of the upright. Using two spacers, one for the length of the mortise and the other for the distance between them, cut the six mortises on each upright. Because these are measured from the top, by means of the spacers, they will not be 'handed', that is, they will not be in pairs, so it is vital that the groove is dead center.

Without adjusting the cutter, cut the grooves for the tenons on the front and back of the horizontal frames. Use the same settings to rout a groove all around the inside of one horizontal frame. This will take the piece of 4mm ($^5/_{32}$in) sycamore which covers the top drawer.

Next, cut the grooves in the 20 × 10mm ($^3/_4$ × $^3/_8$in) vertical frame pieces. Again, use the 4mm ($^5/_{32}$in) cutter and cut to a depth of 4mm ($^5/_{32}$in).

Now change the cutter to a 5mm ($^{13}/_{64}$in) straight cutter and cut the tenons for both horizontal and vertical frames, using a square block of MDF. This will hold the frame piece square to the fence and, because it butts up hard against the frame piece, will prevent tear-out. Without adjusting the cutter, cut the tongues on the 20 × 10mm ($^3/_4$ × $^3/_8$in) pieces of the vertical frames.

Sand the inside faces of the horizontal frames and, using a board with 90° stops and a pair of folding wedges, glue up each of the six frames. As I mentioned above, the top frame has a sycamore panel; this should only be glued in the center at the front and back. Panels should not be glued all the way round as this might prevent the natural movement of the wood; with changes in humidity, in the worst case scenario, the panel could split or the sides be forced apart.

Mark the cross halving joints for all eight corners. Using a radial arm saw or a dovetail saw and chisel, cut a halving joint in the verticals. For the horizontals, make sure the finished length of the top and bottom is equal to the length of the 20 × 10mm ($^3/_4$ × $^3/_8$in) pieces.

Sand the inside faces of all the vertical frames to 400 grit, then glue them up.

Now sand all the remaining faces. If you pin a piece of scrap wood to the bench on either side of the frame, you can sand it using abrasive paper wrapped around a wooden block. Alternatively, if banging veneer pins into your bench doesn't appeal, holding a good thick piece of MDF in a vise will do the same job. If the joints were cut accurately and the pieces are of uniform thickness, it should be possible to sand the frame using 240 grit. However, if there are any major steps between pieces, start with 180 grit, but wrap it around a fairly long piece of wood or you risk sanding the frame unevenly and rounding off the edges. Once you have sanded to 240 grit, you can remove any cross-grain scratches with a piece of folded, 400 grit abrasive, using your thumb to provide pressure and your index finger to prevent it from straying onto the neighboring piece.

Fig 14.5 *Spacing out the drawers*

Fig 14.6 *The vertical frames are all mortised*

Fig 14.7 *The tenon on the drawer support piece*

Fig 14.8 *The corner pieces of a horizontal frame*

Fig 14.9 *The tongue on the horizontal frame*

Fig 14.10 *There is a very tiny shoulder on the corner joint which will neaten up the line*

Fig 14.11 *A board with sliding wedges ensures that the frame is glued up square*

Fig 14.12 *The top horizontal frame*

Fig 14.13 *The cross halving joints on the vertical frame*

Fig 14.14 *Gluing and clamping up the vertical frame*

Fig 14.15 *Sanding the vertical frame flush*

Fig 14.16 *Using the tip of my thumb with a piece of 400 grit abrasive to remove any cross-grain scratch marks*

Fig 14.17 *A little tongue locates the handle*

The drawer handles

The trays, which have been waiting patiently all this time, must now have a groove routed into their fronts to locate the handles. I'm quite sure that glue alone, without any form of joint, would be strong enough to hold them, but with a groove and corresponding tongue in the handle, not only is the joint strengthened, the handles are guaranteed to line up perfectly. Set the stops and fence on the router so that the 4mm ($^5/_{32}$in) cutter cuts stopped grooves slightly over one-third the width of the tray. My fence was set in 46mm ($1^3/_4$in), leaving 86mm ($3^3/_8$in) on the other side. Do remember to rout all the trays from the same side. Believe me, it is possible to cut them from the wrong side. If you're thinking I must have done that, well, you're wrong but I think my guardian angel was with me because I only realized after I had finished that I could have.

Rout a tongue on a 300mm (12in) length of 13 × 10mm ($\frac{1}{2}$ × $\frac{13}{32}$in) bog oak by carefully adjusting the height of the cutter and routing either side to leave a 4 × 3mm ($\frac{5}{32}$ × $\frac{1}{8}$in) tongue. Cut this length into 36mm (1$\frac{7}{16}$in) pieces and chisel the tongue off at the top and bottom.

Sand the sides of the handles with 400mm grit abrasive and glue them onto the trays. It doesn't matter if they're slightly over-length; it's better to sand them off later by rubbing them on an abrasive-covered board or holding them very carefully onto a disc sander. It is just possible to clamp these with two mini sash clamps.

The drawer stops

For the corresponding vertical line at the back, cut a halving joint in the back of each of the drawer supports, with the exception of the top and bottom. The router cutter I used was fractionally small so, rather than adjust the stop, I used a piece of paper folded to get the necessary width. For the top and bottom, rout only halfway through then use a chisel to square off what will, in effect, be half a halving joint. Don't forget that the top and bottom are handed and the stop will need to be adjusted for one of them.

The whole thing can now be glued up. This is a situation in which it's well worth masking the gluing surfaces and oiling and waxing each frame before it is glued up. For one thing, it is very difficult to get into all the corners and finish it properly once it is glued up. For another, it is far easier to remove any glue that has squeezed out, when it has just dried, from a waxed surface than an unwaxed one. And also, it is only after a piece has been oiled that surface scratches show up. While the frames are still separate, something can be done; you can go back a stage and try to remove scratches. With the whole thing glued up it would be a lot more difficult to do this.

Gluing up

Careful preparation is essential. Use the sash clamps for the outside and C-clamps to make sure the horizontal frames are all seated correctly, then use a squaring rod to check, carefully, that the whole thing is square. With the final clamp in place and the final check made, put the phone back on the hook and dish out some serious congratulations – the end is in sight.

Final adjustments and finishing

The next job is to fit the back stop. Cut it precisely to length, insert it into its grooves and mark each of the cross halvings. Cut these to depth with a dovetail or radial arm saw and, if necessary, make any final adjustments, with the piece in position but upside down, by paring with a chisel.

Once you have fitted the back drawer stop, insert the drawers, plane off the handles and finish with 400 grit abrasive wrapped

Fig 14.18 *Cutting the tongue on the handle*

Fig 14.19 *Removing the tongue from the handle*

Fig 14.20 *Gluing the handle in position on the tray*

Fig 14.21 *Using two miniature clamps to hold the handle in place*

Fig 14.22 *Cutting the cross halving joints at the back of the box*

Fig 14.23 *A folded piece of paper is all that's needed to alter the cut*

Fig 14.24 *Horizontal frames with the joints cut for the drawer stops*

Fig 14.25 *Gluing and clamping all the frames together*

Fig 14.26 *Marking the cross halvings onto the drawer stop piece*

Fig 14.27 *Fitting the drawer stop*

Fig 14.28 *Planing the drawer stop flush – with a very sharp plane*

Fig 14.29 *A final sanding of the feet*

around a long piece of wood – long enough for it to never be completely unsupported. If necessary, level off the feet of the box on an abrasive-covered board. And finally, oil and wax all of the remaining un-oiled surfaces.

GALLERY

My friends, my colleagues, my partners in boxmaking. These are some
of the makers out there all over the world beavering away in their
workshops, often on their own, producing fantastic work. Their work has
inspired me, I've learnt from them; in some cases their boxes have made
me smile, in others they have left me open-mouthed in admiration.

*Clare Vetterlein, UK. Ripple
sycamore and purple heart*

*Ross Kaires, Australia. 'Hall of
Elders'. Pinus sp., Eucalyptus sp.,
and bamboo grass*

*Hilary Arnold Baker, UK. Wooden
box. Pine, lacquered gesso with
gessoed muslin binding and
patinated silver leaf*

Jean-Christophe Couradin, France. Rosewood (Palissandre de Madagascar)

*Kim Kelzer, USA, 'Windy'. Painted
basswood*

*Charles B. Cobb, USA. Teapot box.
African zebrawood, walnut*

Christopher Vickers, UK. Jewelry box. Brown oak with enamel heart

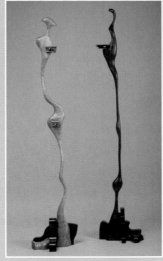 

Chris Cantwell, USA. Tall twisting boxes, and detail. Chakte kok, western maple, wenge, amboyna, burl kingwood

Tom Rauschke and Kaaren Wiken, USA. Black walnut, oak, hickory and fiber embroidery

Martin Lane, UK. Celebration humidor made to commemorate the 150th anniversary of the founding of Harrods Limited of Knightsbridge, London. Bubinga and Kevasingo ebony handles, Belize cedar drawers

Edward L. Love, USA. Ebony and maple

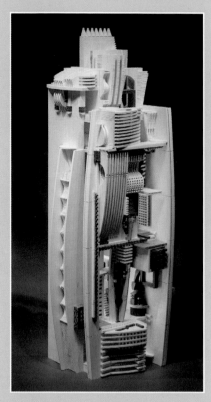

Po Shun Leong, USA. Lamp box in bleached maple

Robert and Andrea Ingham, UK. Top row (l to r): ripple cherry, burr lacewood, burr walnut. Bottom row (l to r): pippy cherry, burr lacewood, weathered ripple sycamore

Michael J. Brolly, USA. 'Thinking of my mother-in-law and those magnificent mahogany breasts'. Mahogany, maple, walnut, cherry, ebony, brass, suede, bearings, magnets and paint

Terry Evans, USA. Ceremonial container. Materials not known

Andrew Crawford, UK. Double-veneered, natural-edged yew on macassar ebony, ebony strapping, maple interior

ABOUT THE AUTHOR

Peter Lloyd's path to becoming a craftsman was by no means a straight one. After working at Heathrow Airport as an air-traffic control assistant, he then changed direction completely and pursued a career in hotel and catering management. Then followed a job in the retail trade, and it was during this period that he began to settle into one direction; to be a craft and design teacher was the goal, reached through part-time study and work as a bench joiner.

Having worked for some years as a secondary school teacher in Cumbria, England, Peter then took up a two-year teaching contract in Botswana, moving there with his wife and two children.

Returning to Cumbria, Peter was now determined to be his own boss. Long ago he'd made a jewelry box for his girlfriend; he had a stunning piece of burr oak and a perfectly serviceable garden shed, and there was a gap in the market – Peter Lloyd Fine Hardwood Boxes was born. Customers and interest gradually started to swell and it was soon time to abandon the shed for a custom-built workshop.

Peter is now firmly established as one of the county's foremost boxmakers. Inspired by the unusual and striking English hardwoods he continuously seeks, he has a passion for boxes. The excitement and enthusiasm with which he creates his gorgeous pieces is self-evident. As well as several solo exhibitions in Europe, his work has been exhibited in some of the best galleries in the UK.

INDEX